LEADERSHIP SECRETS
OF THE
Rogue
Warrior

Photo by Roger Foley

LEADERSHIP SECRETS OF THE
Rogue Warrior

A COMMANDO'S GUIDE TO SUCCESS

by

Richard Marcinko

POCKET BOOKS
New York   London   Toronto   Sydney   Tokyo   Singapore

POCKET BOOKS, a division of Simon & Schuster Inc.
1230 Avenue of the Americas, New York, NY 10020

ISBN: 0-671-54515-9

First Pocket Books hardcover printing June 1996

10 9 8 7 6 5 4 3 2 1

POCKET and colophon are registered trademarks of
Simon & Schuster Inc.

Printed in the U.S.A.

This book is dedicated to a host of key people in my life:

First, and especially, to my talented and dedicated wife, Nancy.

To my "sea daddies," who took the time to raise me, often at the end of their boot.

To my men, "the shooters," who were loyal and followed me.

To my mentors, who were patient and attempted to counsel me.

To my friends and my family, who had to, and continue to, endure me.

To my loyal fans, who dared to ask for this effort.

A special thank-you to Dr. Wayne B. Hanewicz, a close friend, omnipresent mentor, spiritual guru, and Warrior in every sense of the word. He continues to fight battles for the unknown at every front, for almost every cause . . . sainthood still lives in the streets of Ann Arbor. He provided the much-needed research and technical assistance that make this manuscript readable for a larger audience.

Acknowledgments

I want to thank those who have taken the time to make this book an exercise in excellence. These people include:

Paul McCarthy, my editor at Pocket Books, who inspired the idea for this book and saw it through to the end.

Cameron Stauth, who advised me on the book's reorganization and rewriting.

Dan Kuba, Mark DeBeau, and Vince Pettitpren, of the Detroit Metropolitan Wayne County Airport.

Bill Bottum, of Townsend and Bottum, Inc.

Kevin Williams, the dynamic young leader whose success is described in Chapter Three.

Mel Smith and his friends, for recounting the still-developing story of his new academy for kids living in misery.

Finally, my continuing appreciation to the many unsung heroes and Warriors, who constantly demand the *best* of themselves— in relative obscurity.

Contents

The Rogue Warrior's
Ten Commandments of SpecWar*

1. I am the War Lord and the wrathful God of Combat and I will always lead you from the front, not the rear.

2. I will treat you all alike—just like shit.

3. Thou shalt do nothing I will not do first, and thus will you be created Warriors in My deadly image.

4. I shall punish thy bodies because the more thou sweatest in training, the less thou bleedest in combat.

5. Indeed, if thou hurteth in thy efforts and thou suffer painful dings, then thou art Doing It Right.

6. Thou hast not to like it—thou hast just to do it.

7. Thou shalt Keep It Simple, Stupid.

8. Thou shalt never assume.

9. Verily, thou art not paid for thy methods, but for thy results, by which meaneth thou shalt kill thine enemy by any means available before he killeth you.

10. Thou shalt, in thy Warrior's Mind and Soul, always remember My ultimate and final Commandment: There Are No Rules—Thou Shalt Win at All Cost.

* Created by Richard Marcinko and John Weisman, and seen in *Rogue Warrior: Red Cell*, *Rogue Warrior: Green Team*, and *Rogue Warrior: Task Force Blue*, by Richard Marcinko and John Weisman.

LEADERSHIP SECRETS
OF THE
Rogue
Warrior

INTRODUCTION

"I am the Rogue Warrior"

There is no substitute for victory.

—Douglas MacArthur

The essence of leadership is vision. You can't blow an uncertain trumpet.

—Father Theodore Hesburgh

Life is a struggle for survival, for success, and for dominance. Life is war.

It is an economic war. A political war. A social war. And a personal war.

But we are not all warriors.

That is our human failing.

3

It doesn't need to be this way. In all of us—sometimes deeply buried—there beats the heart of a warrior. I want to help you find that heart in yourself. When you find it, you will become a leader—because all true warriors are leaders.

Not all warriors now stand at the head of command, though—not all of them are yet "the boss." But each of them is ready, when the moment arises, to assume that command and to lead the people around them. If a warrior's flag-bearer falls, the warrior is ready to take up the standard and lead the way.

WAR is an acronym: We Are Ready.

I, personally, am a warrior. I live by a warrior's code. I served my country, and served my comrades, for over thirty years in the United States Navy. During this time, I learned how to become a leader. Sometimes the lessons of leadership that I learned were painful, and often they were dangerous. I got my ass kicked in more times than I can count.

In the Navy's Underwater Demolition Teams, I visited some of the prime hellholes on earth. I learned SpecWar— or Special Warfare—from my sea-daddy mentors, who taught me how to not just survive in a hostile environment, but how to thrive. I learned how to destroy my enemies before they destroyed me.

I learned these lessons so well that in Vietnam I was paid the rare compliment of having a price put on my head by the Viet Cong. After that tour, I served in Cambodia, earned a couple of college degrees, and learned the intricacies of counterterrorism and special warfare. After further training, the Pentagon put me in charge of the Navy's first counterterrorist unit, the legendary SEAL Team Six. My swim buddies and I began to roam the globe, searching and destroying the enemies of the American government. We served in Central America, the Middle East, the North Sea, and Africa.

We were so successful that the Navy put me in charge of a unit called Red Cell. Our mission was to become "terrorists" ourselves, to test the security of the Navy's most secure facilities.

Every step of the way, I learned about people: how to motivate their actions, how to inspire them, how to lead them—and how, when necessary, to destroy them.

I assure you, I got one hell of an education. Most valuable of all, it was an education in the real world, in real-time. Even though I hold a master's degree, most of the indispensable lessons I learned came the hard way: while I was in shit up to my hairy eyebrows. I learned what happens when nobody wants to take responsibility for a situation that's completely out of control. I learned how to communicate when nobody wants to listen. I learned how to set goals in the heat of battle and how to devise strategies, revise tactics, and organize men into cohesive units.

As I became a leader, I developed a set of leadership principles. This leadership code was my guiding light. I lived by it. And I was quite prepared to die for it.

Here are the principles that I lived by:

5

The Rogue Warrior's Leadership Code

- I will test my theories on myself first. I will be my own guinea pig.
- I will be totally committed to what I believe, and I will risk all that I have for these beliefs.
- I will back my subordinates all the way when they take reasonable risks to help me achieve my goals.
- I will not punish my people for making mistakes. I'll only punish them for not learning from their mistakes.
- I will not be afraid to take action, because I know that almost any action is better than inaction. And I know that sometimes not acting is the boldest action of all.
- I will always make it crystal clear where I stand and what I believe.
- I will always be easy to find: I will be at the center of the battle.

This code served as my "Commandments for Myself," but, subordinates also need commandments. Thus, The Rogue Warrior's Ten Commandments of SpecWar were created. These "Ten Commandments" were the rules that guided my men.

You have already seen the Ten Commandments earlier in this book, so you know that they are *not* easy to follow. That was their *point*. I did not *want* them to be easy. My missions were deadly and difficult—they were, in fact, some of the most difficult missions that faced the United States armed services. Therefore, I could expect nothing less from my men than total dedication and absolute competence. My expectation of this dedication and competence is embodied in every single word of the Ten Commandments.

Since leaving the U.S. Navy, I have discovered that the Ten Commandments apply not just to military missions, but also to missions in the world of business.

Over the past few years, I have worked as a consultant to many major corporations, and have also been active in the publishing industry, and (to a lesser degree) the entertainment industry. In this book, you will find many anecdotes about the industries that I have been involved with, or have closely observed. I have found that the Ten Commandments apply almost universally to all businesses. Virtually any business leader who follows these Commandments will increase his chances of success.

Of course, I am not the only military man who has learned important lessons during war and then successfully applied these lessons to business. In this book are many examples of former soldiers who later conquered the business world.

If you, in your business, apply these Commandments, you will be able to quickly identify which of your employees are "warriors" and which are stragglers. You'll learn to better understand your employees.

You'll also learn about *yourself*—and that's the most valuable education anyone can get. If you don't understand yourself, you can't possibly understand your mission. If you don't know exactly *why you're on that mission*, and exactly *what you're capable of*, I guarantee you your mission will fail.

I learned that to truly understand yourself and your

mission, you have to confront yourself in the mirror each morning and demand the answers to life's six most difficult questions. These questions (which I'll also address later) are: **What drives me? Was I always this way? What will satisfy me? Do I ever recognize defeat? How can I turn today's negatives into positives? What is my ultimate goal?**

If you can answer each of these questions—*honestly*— at the beginning of each day, you're going to take a giant step closer to being a warrior and a leader. You won't face your day's confrontations with a mind that's mushy with ambivalence, doubt, and confusion. Your focus will be laser-sharp, and you'll pity the poor son of a bitch who tries to stand between you and your goals.

When you achieve this rare state of mind, the people around you will know it. You won't have to yell to get their attention, or "stand on your head" to get their respect. You'll radiate leadership, and people will *want* to follow you.

Think this sounds easy? Think again. It sounds *simple*, and it is simple—but simple is never easy. What's easy is to be so complex, and obtuse, and ambivalent, that nobody even *bothers* to challenge you.

When you approach your life and your goals with simplicity, you naturally draw fire, because you're not hiding behind a wall of obscurity. People know where you stand and what you believe—and, I guarantee you, not all of them are going to like it. If they do, then you've got a big problem—because if everybody agrees with you, you obviously stand for nothing.

That's the problem with so many of today's leaders, in

business and in politics. Their idea of leadership is to take surveys and polls and find out what's popular, and then try to adopt that stance. They want to be all things to all people, and they end up being nothing to nobody. They think popularity is leadership.

But *popularity is not leadership.*

Leadership is taking a position, drawing fire, ducking bullets—and then firing back. You do *that,* and people will follow you.

Your intention may be to just *act like a man,* but the result will be that you'll *act like a leader.*

The path you'll follow will not be easy, but it *will* be the path with heart. Every step of the way, you'll be an obvious target for all the snide little snipers hiding in the bushes. Because you'll be visible, you'll be vulnerable. And because you'll be vulnerable, you'll be very much subject to Murphy's Law. After all, the very nature of Murphy's Law is that it strikes when you can least afford it.

But if you're a warrior, you'll welcome Mr. Murphy, because he'll help keep you honest. He'll make sure you cover every possibility and anticipate every problem. He will call your bluff when you least expect it. Murphy knows that, in some perverse way, he exists because you need him to bring out the best in yourself.

Personally, I get a little disappointed whenever Sir Murphy *doesn't* rear his ugly little head.

When Murphy doesn't show, I lose the opportunity to demonstrate to the men I'm leading that I've prepared for every possibility. And, believe me, preparation is an absolutely critical element of leadership.

9

But even preparation does not lie at the absolute core—the ground zero—of leadership. At the core of leadership is one, single trait: belief in a cause. If you don't believe with all your heart and all your soul in what you're fighting for, you will not be a leader. You will not inspire others to follow you unless you are a man of absolute conviction.

You've got to have a cause. If you aren't fighting for something that's bigger than yourself, you'll be nothing more than just one more ambitious, opportunistic asshole who's trying to claw his way to the top. Personal ambition may motivate *you*, but it's not going to motivate anyone to follow you.

Being a warrior and a leader is not about achieving personal success. Success usually does come to leaders, but to a real leader, personal success is just a secondary gain—a nice payoff, but not the real prize.

The real prize is achieving the victory of a great principle—like freedom, or peace, or the prosperity of the many.

Therefore, a real leader is actually a servant. He's the servant of a great cause.

It's true: Life is war. But if a leader is serving a great cause, he can achieve power. And glory. And fulfillment.

And peace.

CHAPTER ONE

THE FIRST COMMANDMENT

"I am the War Lord and the wrathful God of Combat and I will always lead you from the front, not the rear."

No man is a leader until his appointment is ratified in the minds and hearts of his men.
> —Anonymous, *The Infantry Journal,* 1954

Lead, follow, or get out of the way.
> —Lee Iacocca, Chrysler Corporation

Lead, follow, or get out of my fucking way!
> —R. Marcinko, variation on a theme

You've got to have integrity to be an effective leader. That's what it all stems from.
> —Don Shula, former coach of the Miami Dolphins

The oldest leadership principle—and the most important in existence—is: Lead from the front.

No principle could be more obvious. But no other principle is so abused, and so ignored, by modern leaders.

Like many of the most basic leadership principles, this principle was originally derived from the military—

because the military is the oldest "action institution" in the history of man. In the earliest days of recorded history, leaders invariably led from the front. The great warrior-rulers, from King David to Alexander the Great, rode into battle at the head of their troops. Even leaders like Churchill and Eisenhower were proven warriors, battle-tested. They were willing to take the ultimate risk for the causes in which they believed. And the men they led knew this—that's why these men were willing to follow them.

Too many modern leaders, though—particularly leaders of business—are all too content to rule with the *power of their office*—and not the power of their *courage*, their *beliefs*, their *personality*, and their *intelligence*.

Even worse, a great many business leaders today seem to regard their position as a *refuge* from battle—a "prize" they have won for battles already fought. Their only goal is to hang on to their power, rather than to do something with it. And power that isn't *used* for something is no power at all.

Leading from the front often means literally riding at the head of your troops. In business and in war, you should often be physically in front of your people, seeing what they see, fearing what they fear, and sweating with them as they labor. Some of the great business leaders of our day make it a point to turn off the lights in their own offices only after every other light in the building has gone dim. That way, as their employees go home in the evening, they can see that their leader is still forging ahead, "taking the point."

One of the great business leaders of our era is Lee

Iacocca. No one had to look very hard to find Iacocca during the Chrysler comeback. He could be found on the production line, in high-level and low-level meetings, at the White House, and in Congress. He made it legitimate again for CEOs to personally vouch for their products. This was leadership.

But being physically present at the "front lines" isn't the only way to lead from the front. As a leader, you should *symbolically* stay at the forefront of every major battle. Even if you're stuck at headquarters, you should let your people in the field know that you're with them in spirit. That means knowing exactly what they need, and getting it to them. It means keeping in constant contact with them—by phone, fax, E-mail, and modem. In fact, today's superb communications systems—which the great warrior-leaders of the past would have *loved*—offer unparalleled opportunities for leaders to be in the thick of every corporate battle.

When you lead your people from the front, you do more than just inspire them to follow you. You also inspire *them* to be leaders. For every major leader in a company, there may be a dozen midlevel managers—or even production-line workers—who rise to a position of leadership in a crisis. Your company will only be as strong as its weakest links, and if you train even your "weak links" to be tough, your company will flourish. If you do this, when one leader "falls"—from illness, or accident, or age—another will immediately take his place.

But this can only happen in organizations that are not straitjacketed by bureaucracy, rigid status hierarchies, and overspecialization of jobs. A company will be able to adjust to crisis only if it's the type of company where employees are flexible about the work they do. In a crunch, nonmanagers should be able to manage, and leaders should be able to roll up their sleeves and do the grunt work.

Great leaders are never afraid to help out "on the line." You see this when a police chief volunteers to work the midnight shift. You see it when a CEO answers the phones when his secretary is overwhelmed. You see it when a teacher is willing to learn from a student.

When a leader takes over the job of a subordinate, one of the things he often learns is that he's not as good at the job as the subordinate. Nothing wrong with that! You don't *have* to be as good as your subordinates. You just have to be willing to take the same risks that you ask them to take. If you can't lead with your body, you can lead with your heart.

Another thing that happens when you lead from the front is that your people see exactly how you feel about every issue. It defines your character. And as your character becomes clear to your subordinates, it's easier for them to predict your desires, your reactions, and your behavior. They won't have to be mind readers to know what you want. Then, when they manage on their own, they'll know how *you* would have solved their problems.

Of course, every time you reveal your character, you take the chance that your subordinates will find your character to be lacking. If you're a true leader, you'll let them tell you, and you'll take their advice to heart. Then you'll change—and continue to succeed.

If you lead from the front, you'll find out almost

immediately if you actually have the *legitimacy* to lead. Too often, people in power just assume that because they are the "leader," everyone will treat them accordingly. But it is one thing to occupy the position of leader and quite another to have the legitimacy to lead. When legitimacy is missing, the leader will find out the hard way that no one is following. This kind of "leader" will soon see that he's no leader at all.

Without legitimacy, you can only lead by fear. And fear simply will not enable you to command people who are strong and self-confident.

I, for one, have *never* allowed myself to be led by fear, because fear is something that I simply will not succumb to. I recognize it, I understand its impact, but I will not allow it to be my motivator. I will allow myself to be led only by a legitimate leader.

To acquire legitimacy, you must stand for something. And that something has to be more than just your own self-interest. You must stand for principles, ideas, and the needs of others. A warrior always stands for something greater than himself. In the end, a warrior is always a noble servant for a noble cause.

That noble cause doesn't have to be abstract or complex or lofty. It can be something as simple as survival. Or it can be the success of a company that supports a number of families.

But just *believing* in the cause doesn't make you the leader. A lot of people believe in things. But are they willing to sacrifice, and sweat, and risk their lives for their cause? Probably not. But a leader *is* willing. And that's what gives him legitimacy.

17

If you are going to lead people who have strong and independent spirits, you can do it only because they have *allowed* you to be their leader. You must *work* for the respect of your team, and you must *earn* your legitimacy from them. You must win their hearts and minds, if you are to lead them into battle.

There is no better way to win their hearts and minds—and to earn your legitimacy—than by leading from the front. It demonstrates that you are ready to give *to* them everything that you ask *from* them.

Few have ever stated this principle better than Major A. C. Bach, in his 1917 farewell address to the graduating officers at Fort Sheridan, Wyoming.

In that address, Major Bach said,

> When you join your organization, you will find there a willing body of men who ask from you nothing more than the qualities that will command their respect, their loyalty, and their obedience. They are perfectly ready and eager to follow you, so long as you can convince them you have those qualities. When the time comes that they are satisfied you do not possess them, you might as well kiss yourself good-bye.
>
> Your usefulness is at an end.

The Rogue Warrior Mentality: Lessons from War

It was the monsoon season in Cambodia, 1973, and the dreaded Khmer Rouge were in control of much of the countryside. In the capital city of Phnom Penh, though, life was still soft—at least, it was soft for the upper echelon of the Khmer Republic government and military personnel. And that's the way they wanted to keep it. Even the midlevel military fighting men didn't want to go in-country and mix it up with the Khmer Rouge. Who would?

Well . . . I did. That's how I am. Officially, as the new naval attaché in the Khmer Republic, I was tasked with giving advice and nothing more. But that's not how I lead. I don't think you can "advise" the men under you to do what you, yourself, are unwilling—or unable—to do. That's not leadership. That's just hollow power, and that kind of power never lasts. If you "lead" that way, the second your men get out of your sight, they're going to do whatever they damn well please. And you can bet it's not going to be what you "ordered" them to do.

For decades, the French had been the advisers to the Cambodians. The French had lived the colonial good life, quitting early in the day to suck down cocktails on their verandas as their servants scurried around. They'd become so isolated and so insulated from reality that they probably thought they could exist happily as colonial aristocracy until the end of time. But then Dien Bien Phu had brought doom on them all—and rightly so.

When I'd first arrived in Phnom Penh, the Cambodian military hierarchy ensconced me in the nicest Luxury Trap they could find—a gardened estate replete with servants—and I'm sure they fully expected me to tuck my tail between my legs and cause no problems.

But I was there as a warrior, not a houseguest, and the

next thing they knew, I was personally leading patrols into the bush. Of the 396 days I spent in Phnom Penh, I was in combat for 291 of them.

The Khmer Army bigwigs rewarded my willingness to take risks with an attitude that was a mixture of contempt and genuine puzzlement. They didn't want their *own* well-fed butts to be within a hundred kilometers of any messy engagement with the enemy. And they probably wondered why the men serving under them regarded them as nothing much more than excess baggage.

But a few of the Khmer Republic military men were true warriors. They knew what life would be like if the Khmer Rouge took over. If you happened to see the movie *The Killing Fields, you* know what it was like when the Khmer Rouge *did* take over.

These warriors—all potential leaders—were few in number, and many of them were just enlisted men. But it didn't matter to me that they weren't all high-ranking officers. You don't have to be the Boss to lead; you just have to be a leader. The source of these warriors' power wasn't their rank; it was their belief in what they were fighting for. That gave them all the legitimacy to lead that they needed.

My job, as I saw it, was to increase the number of true warriors in the Khmer Republic military. So that's what I was trying to do.

One night I remember well—a night so wet with monsoon you could damn near drown standing up—I went out on patrol with a Khmer lieutenant commander, two lieutenants, and a dozen enlisted men. At first, the officers had wanted to just send the men out, but I assured them that there was no way in hell that that was going to happen. I told them I was going out *myself*, and that I wanted the best men available to back me up—meaning, them. I stroked them and cajoled them. I told them they'd be missing all the fun if they didn't come. I could have been a hard-ass about it, but there was no point in just enforcing my will on them; my job was to instill in them a will of their own. When they went with me—and they *would* go with me—I wanted them to think it had been their idea.

Finally, we reached a meeting of the minds and loaded our PBR (Patrol Boat, River) with about forty pounds of explosives. We headed up the Mekong River to visit doom and death on a Khmer Rouge ambush site. The Mekong River was our major supply route, and the Khmer Rouge were playing hell with it. They were attacking our boats with impunity. There was a partly submerged landing craft in the river that forced our ships to sail close to the riverbank—where the VC lay in ambush.

Just outside the city, our PBR drew fire. The officers wanted to cut and run. I overruled them, fired a flare in the direction of our attackers, and started blasting away with the PBR's .50-caliber machine gun. But I wasn't there for my own fun; I was there to teach these people to lead— so I handed off the gun to one of the officers. He whaled away and the attack stopped. That's one of the rules of combat: attack, attack, attack. No defense like a good offense. When the attack stopped, the officer looked happy. He was *learning*—learning that it was more fun to attack than to be attacked and learning that if you put up a fight, you're not going to be quite so easy to kill.

21

An hour later, we arrived at the ambush site. I hit the partly submerged wreck with a spotlight. Silence. No Khmer Rouge tonight.

It was time for somebody to attach the explosives to the wreck. That somebody was me. Theoretically, I could have delegated, but what would that have taught? That the way to win a war is to let somebody else do your dirty work?

I went over the side with the explosives. Strong current. Poor visibility. But I got the explosives attached to the bow. I went back down to attach the timer. And then— just because this was when I *least* wanted it to—Murphy's Law went into action. I sliced up my arm on the keel. One of the charges came loose. As I fiddled with it, I cut myself again. Checked everything. Double-checked. Then I pulled a fuse to start the timer. Nothing. I used my backup. It worked; the fuse ignited. Thank God for backups. They're your best line of defense against Sir Murphy.

I poked my head above water. *Zing! Plop!* Bullets. The Khmer Rouge were back. And my boat was gone.

What fun! Within seven minutes, forty pounds of C-3 explosives were going to launch me to the treetops. I was taking fire from both banks. And there was no sign whatsoever of my PBR.

But a few minutes later—minutes that didn't *seem* like minutes—my boat came gurgling back. I'd shown the officers some balls, and now *they* were showing some balls. They steered straight into the gunfire. I ignored the gunshots and swam on the surface like a piranha out of hell.

I flopped aboard and we roared off. *Bramm!* The explosives blew. The shock rocked our boat into the air.

But the officers, by now, were *galvanized*. By the time we got back to Phnom Penh, they weren't acting the same, and they didn't even look the same. Now, they respected me, and they respected themselves.

They'd gone out on that patrol as civil servants—and they'd come back as warriors.

That's what happens when you lead from the front.

That, of course, wasn't the only time that I led my men from the front. I made a *habit* of it, and that's why my men would follow me to hell and back.

When they followed me, they weren't just following the insignias on my uniform. They were following *me*, personally. They knew that if I asked them to do something, it wasn't because I was too scared, or too lazy, or too arrogant, to do it myself. They knew that I was asking them because I *believed* in the mission at hand. That, and that alone, gave me my legitimacy and my authority.

In Vietnam, when my primary patrol "point man," James "Patches" Watson, needed a break, I'd be the one who took over for him. And the benefit I got out of that wasn't just gaining the loyalty of my men. When I literally "took the point," I could make decisions instantly, without having to interpret the hand signals of someone else. Reaction time was minimized, and all actions were expedited. More important, I learned the pressures and the responsibilities that Jim Watson faced every day. And when I better understood the job of my right-hand man, I understood my own job better, too.

When I was working counterterrorist ops in Beirut, I

also "took the point." Before I let my men come into that godforsaken combat zone, I went in myself for a few days and operated solo. I got the lay of the land, figured out who needed to be paid off and how much to pay them, and found places for my men to live that were safe—at least, "safe" by the standards of Beirut.

Then, when my men did come in, they came in with a feeling of confidence, and the knowledge that whatever they faced, I'd faced, too—and faced *first*.

That's what made these men willing to come to a place like Beirut. They could be sure that I was covering them from in front.

And I could be sure that they were covering my back.

The Rogue Warrior Mentality: Lessons from Business

Lee Iacocca is one of the true warriors of the modern business world. He leads from the front. It's the only way he knows.

When most people think of how Iacocca saved the Chrysler Corporation from bankruptcy, they think it was the loans he got from the government that were the key to that company's survival. But the loans weren't the solution.

The key to the company's turnaround was a series of wage rollbacks that Iacocca instituted. He saved *hundreds of millions* of dollars for the company, by demanding that virtually everyone at Chrysler work for less money. He cut his executives' salaries by ten percent, which had never happened before in the auto industry. And then he killed their stock incentive plan.

Then, one night, he had a showdown with the union. He went to their meeting and delivered a one-minute speech. He told them that he had thousands of jobs available for seventeen dollars an hour, but none at the twenty-dollar level that they *had* been getting. He gave them just that one night to make up their minds: Take it or leave it. But if you leave it, he told them, I'm going to declare bankruptcy in the morning.

They took it.

How come? Because they were desperate? No. They took it because Iacocca had announced to them that he'd *already* cut his own salary. To one dollar per year. So when it came time for them to vote on their own pay cut, they didn't like it—but they knew they should take it. They knew that the boss had already made an even bigger sacrifice than they were being asked to make and that allowed them to swallow the pay cut. It hurt them in their pocketbooks, but it didn't hurt their pride, and it didn't hurt their spirit. They knew that *everybody* up and down the organizational chart was suffering. They knew this wasn't just another trick by management to fleece them out of their hard-earned pay.

Iacocca's leadership from the front inspired people other than just his own troops. Remember those ads Frank Sinatra made for Chrysler? Sinatra said that if his buddy Lee could work cheap to save the company, he could, too. Sinatra's pay was also one dollar.

When Bill Cosby heard what Iacocca was doing—and what Iacocca's people were doing—Cosby came to town and put on a show for twenty thousand Chrysler employees. And he didn't even demand his dollar.

The whole image of Chrysler started to change. No longer was Chrysler just another fat American car company that didn't give its customers as much for their money as the foreign car companies. Now Chrysler was the underdog, the little guy that refused to die. People started buying Chryslers again.

Iacocca, as you can see, didn't just talk the talk; he walked the walk. He took the point, his people fell in behind him, and they won their battle.

General Motors, incidentally, saw what Iacocca had done, and the leader of that company, Roger Smith, tried to mimic Chrysler's success. He asked his workers to give up massive amounts of their pay. And he announced that he would cut his *own* million-dollar compensation package . . . by a whopping $1,620 per year.

Lee Iacocca ended up being a modern American hero. Roger Smith ended up being the butt of the scathing documentary *Roger and Me*. Moral of story: You can't fake leadership. You lead, you follow, or get out of the way.

You don't have to be as famous as Lee Iacocca to lead from the front. And you don't always have to make grand, dramatic gestures to fortify your command.

When Charles Cumello, the former CEO of Waldenbooks, took over that company, it was sucking mud. The book business is a tough arena by any standard, and in 1991 the entire industry was slumping—and Waldenbooks was getting its ass kicked by its competitors.

When Cumello took the helm, Waldenbooks was trying to capture its market share by having the widest selection and the most books of any chain. Wasn't working. They were getting excellent foot-traffic, but their ratio of sales per customer just wasn't cutting it. Customers were looking but not buying.

Cumello, six months new to the job—a virtual virgin— wanted to do something about converting traffic to sales. He didn't know *what* to do, but, by God, he was going to do *something*, and if that didn't work, he'd do something else.

To figure out what to do, he bailed out of corporate HQ and dived into the trenches. He started working the cash registers at a number of Waldenbooks outlets.

Once he was actually in the front lines, he could clearly identify the primary problem. Customer service. Customers were wandering in—and wandering out—in a veritable daze, overwhelmed by the wide selection that had initially attracted them. To change that, Cumello instituted a new policy: Every store employee had to address *every customer within ten feet,* and help them find what they wanted.

Cumello went back to HQ and waited six months to see the shake-out.

The results were . . . nothing. Zilch. Sales stayed flat.

For Cumello, it was back to the bush. He hit his stores again, to find out why the new strategy wasn't working. And he found out.

The store executives—the managers and assistant managers—were telling their clerks to carry out the policy, but the executives weren't taking part in the program themselves. Hustling customers, one by one, was beneath their dignity. Not worth their very important time.

And what message did that send to the floor-level clerks? That the policy didn't really matter. So *nobody* was doing it—at least, not with any zest or conviction.

Cumello started going store to store again and showing every clerk—and every manager and assistant manager—exactly how he wanted them to approach each customer. Day after day, Cumello hustled books, one-on-one. What could the managers say? When you see the CEO of your company dragging his ass around your store, hyping books one at a time, it's pretty hard to think it's beneath your dignity to do it yourself.

Word about what Cumello was doing got around to every store in the chain—and that was no accident, either. Even though Cumello couldn't hit the "front lines" of every outlet, he *could* let them know what he was doing through his company's internal communications system.

In short order, every manager in the company knew exactly where Cumello stood on this issue. And they sure as hell knew what *they* were expected to do.

Managers started complying with the policy. And that made the assistant managers comply. And that made the clerks comply. The domino theory.

By the end of the next quarter, sales figures started to balloon. The sales-per-customer ratio grew. Soon, there was a significant increase in regular customers.

By 1993 the company had done an about-face on the customer service issue. By then, customer surveys ranked Waldenbooks as the industry leader in customer service. Overall sales figures rocketed upward. Profits soared.

All this happened because Charlie Cumello had acted

like a Rogue Warrior, and had led from the front. He'd found his company's problem, he'd figured out how to fix it, he'd told his managers how to fix it, he'd kicked some butts when they'd refused to fix it, and then he'd rewarded them when they *had* fixed it.

That's leadership. Rogue Warrior leadership.

CHAPTER TWO

THE SECOND COMMANDMENT

*"I will treat you all alike—
just like shit."*

Before God, we're all equally wise, and equally foolish.
                                    —Albert Einstein

All men are created equal.

                                    —Thomas Jefferson

In the Navy, I believed in treating everyone equally—just like shit.

But after somebody *proved himself* to me, I adjusted my attitude accordingly. I then treated him like a colleague—like a fellow warrior.

To me, making someone prove himself is pure democracy. It's the American way. It's good management. And it's good sense.

But unfortunately, that attitude is rare today in American business. These days, it's considered . . . rude . . . to demand that a business associate or a subordinate prove himself. You're supposed to just give the guy the benefit of the doubt. Otherwise, you might *hurt his feelings.*

In business today, most employees think they don't *need* to prove themselves. They think their "track record" speaks for itself, and that they have no obligation to "jump through hoops" for you.

The business community is now *full* of prima donnas and narcissists, all filled with lofty expectations about what *you* can do for *them.*

What a sad goddamn irony it is that America, the world's greatest experiment in self-governing, self-responsible democracy, has become a nation of narcissists. The fruits of our fathers' labor—the big payoff for our national success—is that, as a country, we've decided that we're now just *too damn good* to do the dirty work that it takes to prove ourselves.

Do you think the managers in emerging second-world and third-world countries are unwilling to prove themselves? Hell, no, they're not, and that's why we're scared to death of them. They're willing to dig in and do whatever it takes to succeed. Unless we execute an about-face of our national attitude, these little pissant countries are going to blow right by us after the turn of the century. America may well end up the way the British did in *this* century: passed by, undeservedly pompous, and mystified that the Empire disintegrated so quickly.

Right now in America, neither the managerial class *nor* the working class are willing to prove their worth *before* they demand their reward.

We've now got a managerial class that thinks the world owes them a Mercedes, and a working class that thinks the world owes them a pickup truck.

Our managerial class now leads from "on high," and doesn't even want to *hear* about the problems of its workers. The current crop of managers thinks that "toughness" just means downsizing, and simply *insisting* that the peons who survive the layoffs do all the work that needs to be done. Most of today's managers are so self-involved, and so self-congratulatory, that they no longer even see their workers as individuals. To them, the workers are just interchangeable parts in the vast bureaucracy of production.

And how do the workers respond to this attitude? They respond with contempt, of course. When your manager sees you as a "thing," you see him as an asshole. He doesn't care about your problems, so you don't care about his.

The idea of loyalty to the company has gone out the window—because the company is no longer loyal to the worker. When a worker feels like he's a cog in a machine, he doesn't act like a self-reliant, self-responsible *individual*. He acts like a petulant, grievance-laden, demanding *dependent*. He wants full *benefits*. He wants a lifelong *pension*. He wants total job security. He wants a fat 401-K. He wants a month off every year. In short, he no longer wants to be your employee, he wants to be your *child*.

The way I see it, the company doesn't owe its managers new Mercedes, and it doesn't owe its workers new pickups. Nobody owes *anybody anything*.

Your company owes you something only when you *perform*. You've got to *earn* your worth through your *actions*. Until you do that, you're nothing—you're just another child whining for attention. When my Navy subordinates acted like that, I gave them a little "maturity counseling"—with the toe of my *boot*.

These days, in my business affairs, I *still* don't care if you were born a king or a peasant: My kingdom is still a meritocracy, and your *actions* are the only things that count in my eyes.

How will you feel when I make you prove your worth to me? At first, you'll probably be pissed off. You won't *like* having to prove yourself. It's *hard*. But when you do, you're going to feel better than you have in a long time. You're going to experience a feeling of self-worth that you may not have felt for years. And that feeling is going to empower you beyond your wildest dreams. You're going to feel like somebody who's ready to kick ass and take names. You'll feel *sorry* for the punk who tries to stand between you and your goals.

And I'll tell you something else in you that will change: your outlook toward others. You'll stop judging them by what they *are*, and start judging them by what they *do*. And *that* will change *them*.

When this happens, you'll take another step closer to being a true leader of real warriors.

The Rogue Warrior Mentality: Lessons from War

I was in a chopper, hovering above the greasy and warm Suez Canal, giving last-minute instructions to an Egyptian Army Ranger named Captain Hadj.

SEAL Team Six was in Egypt to train that country's elite squad of counterterrorist commandos. Problem was, President Mubarak's "elite" Army Rangers were a bunch of fat-assed misfits and dullards. They couldn't shoot, they fought like sissies in dresses, and their motivation was approximately on a par with that of someone in a coma.

Worst of all, their command structure was patterned on the archaic caste system of princes and peasants. The caste system was a vestige of the old days, when the British Empire had ruled Egypt, and had conferred power only upon a small class of corrupt elites.

The Egyptian officers I was working with, like Captain Hadj, were upper-class political appointees who thought they'd been anointed at birth with special rights. They did not believe they had to prove themselves to their own men, or to us American advisers. Therefore, they never did much of *anything*.

The *enlisted* men were also hamstrung by the rigid social order. They were stuck at the bottom of the dung-heap, and they were doomed to stay there *forever*, no matter how hard they worked, or how brave they were. So they didn't go out of their way to distinguish themselves by their actions. They had no incentive.

The officers treated the enlisted men like untouchables.

They ordered them around as if they were servants, rather than subordinates (and if you haven't realized by now that I think there's a *big* difference between servants and subordinates, you've wasted your money on this book). The officers didn't *lead* their men, they just *directed* them. Therefore, there *was* no direction.

Captain Hadj, who was piloting the chopper, was supposed to lower me into a speeding boat, down below, as I dangled from a "caving ladder." We were teaching the Egyptian Rangers how to do that trick. It's a tough maneuver, a helluva lot harder to do than it looks in James Bond movies. If you don't calibrate the speed between the copter and the boat perfectly, the dangle-ee ends up with an outboard propeller up his ass. Or he ends up water-skiing behind a helicopter—with no skis.

Skippering the speedboat was one of my best men, Lieutenant J.G. Rod Blake—aka "Ramrod"—who'd served with me in Vietnam and various other garden spots of the Orient. My calculation was, whatever expertise and motivation I lost with Captain Hadj, I'd get back with Ramrod. At least, that was the *idea*.

As I shouted last-minute instructions to Hadj, he tweaked his glossy mustache distractedly. The supercilious son of a bitch was more worried about trying to look like Omar Sharif than in keeping my poor ass out of harm's way. As I got a grip on the ladder, Hadj fiddled with the gold buttons on his custom-made flight suit. I snarled at him to pay attention to his work, but he didn't even look up. He was a prize prima donna, and he couldn't have cared less what I thought of him. As far as he was concerned, he *had it made,* and didn't have to prove anything to anybody.

We zoomed in over the boat, and they began to lower me down.

Below, Ramrod's spotter yelled instructions into his ear, as Rod barreled down the canal, occasionally glancing over his shoulder at me.

In less than a minute, I was only a few feet above the water and a few feet behind the boat. I began to reach for outstretched hands from the speedboat.

Then suddenly, for some reason—because of wind, or maybe just plain stupidity—Hadj cut his speed.

Next thing I knew, Ramrod was cutting *his* speed—which was a no-no. He was supposed to maintain an even velocity and let the aircraft catch up.

I smacked the back of the boat hard, bounced off, and crashed into the water. I skipped across the surface like a flat rock. There's a technique to that maneuver, but it's mostly instinct. At that speed, you're basically just trying to keep the water from pulling off your arms and legs.

When we mustered back at base camp, I pulled Ramrod and Hadj out of formation and chewed them out. It was just a standard ass-chewing: You stupid, goddamn, pus-sucking, pencil-dick, shit-for-brains, morons! And so on and so forth. The usual chatter.

Ramrod took his whippin' like a man, and it was forgotten—we got together later that night and drank about fourteen Stella beers.

But Captain Hadj apparently wasn't *accustomed* to having naughty words directed at him, because he started to *sass* me. Which was not a bright thing to do, since my whole body was still burning from my belly flop.

So I hauled off and slapped the shit out of him.

He looked at me in utter disbelief. The eyes of his enlisted men got bigger and bigger, until I was afraid their eyeballs were going to pop right out of their heads and go rolling across the tarmac.

Then I just dismissed them all and walked away.

I'd made my point: I don't care *who* you are—I don't care if you're King Farouk's favorite grandson—if you work for me, I'll judge you by what you *do*, and how well you do it. I don't care who you *are*, or who you *know*. I don't play favorites.

Hadj had fucked up, and jeopardized my life, so in my book, he was lower than camel shit at the bottom of a dry well.

For the next six months, that's how I treated him.

Gradually, his enlisted men got the message: This guy was *nothing*—just an empty uniform.

Over the next six months, Hadj's enlisted men began to act like soldiers, instead of servants. Following my pattern, they started to treat Hadj with thinly veiled contempt.

The Egyptian enlisted men shifted their loyalties to me. They took risks, and proved themselves. Pretty soon, some of them were true warriors. I was proud of those men, and let them know it. Two of them, with great difficulty, later became officers.

Not long after I left, Hadj helped direct the antiterrorist unit that stormed a hijacked Egyptian plane in Malta. In that ill-conceived operation, fifty-seven hostages were killed.

Hadj was called on the carpet for his role in the bungled operation. He asked two of his enlisted men to cover his ass and say he'd been blameless.

They told him to go to hell.

Hadj was drummed out of the service.

If Hadj had been smart, he would have learned his lesson the "easy" way, on the day I slapped his face.

But punks like him never learn. They think they're better than everyone else—right up until the day their own narcissism destroys them.

The Rogue Warrior Mentality: Lessons from Business

In 1896 a hot young businessman got a job as a cash-register salesman for the National Cash Register Company of Buffalo, New York. But this kid was just lousy at selling cash registers. He delivered the same canned speech to every potential customer, but none of them swallowed it. In his first two weeks, he didn't make a single sale.

The kid had a big ego, because he'd already had a little success as a salesman and as a butcher-shop owner. So he had a hard time accepting the fact that he couldn't sell cash registers. He thought someone, somehow, should make things easier for him.

He went whining to his boss. But the boss just *exploded.* Went ballistic. He started ripping the kid apart. The boss, a tough old man named Jack Range, yelled at the kid in words *cats and dogs* could understand. He knew the kid had a tender ego—but Range just didn't *care.* He was truly

41

democratic: he gave shit to everyone. The only way anyone could get off Jack Range's shit list was to prove himself.

The kid was livid. He fully intended to tell the old man to go to hell—as soon as he could get a word in edgewise.

But as the screaming continued, the kid realized: *This guy's right. I'm screwing up, and I've got no one to blame but myself.* The kid held his tongue and absorbed the lesson.

Then the kid and the old man went out together, and the old man taught the kid how to improvise on the canned speech. It was the old man's philosophy that even though a boss should be tough as hell, he should still be an *assistant* to the men who worked for him.

With the old man's assistance, the kid made his first sale. The old man stayed with the kid until the young man had made several more sales.

Pretty soon, the kid became one of the top salesmen in the company. Not long thereafter, the kid was running his own small company. Before his career was over, the kid—Thomas Watson, Sr.—had changed American business forever with his new little company, called International Business Machines, or IBM.

Midway through Watson's career, he brought his son, Tom Watson, Jr., into the business. On his son's first day in the office, the father took him to see a midlevel manager. Watson said to his son, "Tom, you've met Charley Kirk." Then he told his son that he was going to be Kirk's *assistant*. Tom Watson, Jr., was stunned. He had expected to start in the *executive* ranks. But that's not how his father ran IBM. Watson, Sr., had learned a lesson from old Jack

Range: Every man has to *prove* himself. Even the boss's son.

Tom Watson, Jr., had enough sense not to bitch about having to prove himself to his own father. If he had, his father might well have fired him on the spot. Watson, Sr., was tough, caustic, and outspoken—a true Rogue Warrior.

It took Watson, Jr., several days to get over his shock. He felt better, though, after he realized that at IBM, "assistant" didn't mean "lackey." In fact, Watson, Sr., insisted that all of his managers consider themselves assistants to the men who worked *under* them.

There was a status hierarchy at IBM, but it wasn't one that was determined by position. It was determined by action and by accomplishment.

Tom Watson, Jr., eventually took over IBM, and made it one of the most legendary companies in America. *Fortune* magazine would later call him "the most successful capitalist in history."

Tom Watson, Jr., was just as straightforward, outspoken, and demanding as his father had been. He made sure IBM remained a meritocracy. He wasn't afraid to confront anybody, anytime. He had a sharp tongue and could bite the ass off a bear.

Once, when he was ranting at someone in a meeting, one of his vice presidents asked another v.p., "Do you know why they all take this bunk from him?"

"Why?"

"Because they're all getting *filthy rich!*"

The Watsons treated everyone alike. And no businessmen ever ran a company better.

CHAPTER THREE

THE THIRD COMMANDMENT

"Thou shalt do nothing I will not do first, and thus will you be created Warriors in My deadly image."

I will not send troops to danger which I will not myself encounter.
                              —The Duke of Marlborough

Been there. Done that. Now you go there and do that!
                              —Richard Marcinko

I used to say, "Go boldly in among the English," and then I used to go boldly in myself.
                              —Joan of Arc

Example is leadership.
                              —Albert Schweitzer

You know that phrase, "Do as I say, not as I do"? Try leading men into battle with that attitude. If you try that, you'd better bring along a mirror, so that you can watch your own ass—because nobody behind you will be watching it.

Too many "leaders" today talk about teamwork, but

they define the team as their *subordinates*—with themselves, as the leader, set apart.

If you're the leader, but you aren't *part* of the team, then *you've got no team.* What you have is a *bureaucracy.* And even if it's a small bureaucracy, it's going to function like a bureaucracy: not very well.

Commitment from your people isn't something that can be demanded from them; it can only be *given* by them. And your team will give their commitment to you only if they know that *you'll* do whatever you're asking *them* to do.

Remember, all great leaders fight not for themselves, but for their cause. And most of their subordinates are pretty much the same. The subordinates' *main* loyalty is to the cause, not the leader. Therefore, if your team members see that you're not willing to sacrifice *everything* for the cause, they won't want to follow you. They'll follow someone who'll put his money where his mouth is.

If you take the attitude of "You go first," you won't be the leader. You'll just be the boss, the lucky son of a bitch who somehow grabbed the power.

As I mentioned earlier, your cause doesn't have to be altruistic and abstract. You don't have to be fighting to end world hunger. You can just be fighting to keep your company from going tits-up. That's a *great* cause—if it's keeping you and your employees out of the unemployment lines.

If you *do* want your team to "do as you do," then your only possible course of action is to get your ass out in front of them and *do* something. Maybe that will mean spending a couple of hours on the production floor, packing boxes, if you need to get out a crucial shipment. Maybe it will mean joining the secretaries to lick envelopes, if you need to get out an important mailing. Obviously, you *could* call a temp agency for either of these jobs. But if you do that, you'll lose a hell of a good opportunity to send some important messages to your people.

One of the messages is that what they're doing is *important.* Another is that you don't consider yourself *better* than them. Another is that you now know, first-hand, how hard their jobs are. When you send these messages—with your actions, instead of your mouth— you'll inspire your people not just to do their *own* jobs better, but to do someone else's job, too, if the need arises.

If you're a smart leader, you'll look for ways to occasionally get out on the production floor. If your people actually see you sweat, it'll build morale faster than any bonus system you could possibly enact.

If you regularly do this kind of hands-on work, you'll not only build your *team's* morale, you'll also build your *own* morale. Sitting in the big corner office and playing President is nice, but it's not what you *started out* doing, is it? You probably started out somewhere down on the floor, getting your hands dirty, and staying close to your product. When you left that hands-on level, you lost something. You lost that gut-level satisfaction you used to get from doing simple things well. You also lost your close involvement with your product. And if you're a true business-world warrior, you *love* your product. It's your baby. Even if it's just toilet seats that you make, you *love* toilet seats. You know everything about them—their specs, their designs, even their goddamn *history.*

As you rose through the ranks, though, and lost touch with your product, you also lost touch with part of *yourself.*

Even if you joined your current company at a high executive level, I'm sure there was a time in your career when you were a hands-on guy.

Be advised: A real leader never fully leaves behind what he used to do. Instead, he *incorporates* all his old skills, and his old relationships, into his new jobs.

I know a wealthy publisher—a guy who started out in the mailroom—who still prides himself on his photocopying skills. Yes, *photocopying.* Sounds pretty simple, right? Any numb-nuts can push the "on" button, right? Well, this guy can tell you exactly *where* to grab the paper to get it out of the machine fastest, *how* to operate two machines at once, and on and on. Sometimes he goes down to the mailroom just to keep his proficiency up. That may sound extreme to you. But this guy has not just the best *mailroom* in the business, but the most efficient, all-around *company* in the business. On his way up, he did a little of everything—PR, sales, editing, and production. He was good at all of it, and he still likes doing all of it. So he's all over the building, all the time.

His company runs like a Swiss watch—because it doesn't just have a boss at the top, it has a *leader.*

The Rogue Warrior Mentality: Lessons from War

In the Navy, I didn't become a leader by becoming an officer. I became an officer by being a leader. I'll tell you about something I did just *before* I left for OCS—Officer Candidate School (or Organized Chicken Shit, as I prefer).

During my last few days as an enlisted man, I was working with a group of seamen in the Mediterranean, and our training mission was to learn High Altitude Low Opening parachute jumps. In a HALO jump, you bail out about five miles above the earth, then free-fall until you're 1,800 to 1,000 feet from the ground. Then, and only then, do you open your chute. Of course, if your timing isn't perfect, you go splat, and end up wearing a halo in heaven.

The purpose of a HALO jump is to minimize the time that you're a target for the ground forces below.

For some reason, the men I was with were a little squeamish about the exercise—partly because we were doing it over the open seas. Parachuting into water meant that we also had to factor drowning into the equation. I didn't worry about drowning, though: hell, the *fall* was going to kill us.

When we were aloft, with our chutes on our backs, everybody was sort of looking at everybody else, like, "Who wants to die *first?*" Since this was practically my last day before OCS, I could've just lagged behind and gone last, so that nobody would really notice if I opened my chute at a safer, higher altitude.

But, me being me, that wasn't going to happen. I had a plan. I was going to show these people exactly *why* they would soon be saluting me as an officer, and why I would *deserve* that salute. I lurched to the front of the line, gave everybody a big shit-eating grin, and announced my intentions.

"Gentlemen," I said, "I am now going to demonstrate the proper HALO technique, by deploying my chute at the *masthead level of our ship*." They all looked at me like, "Good *luck*, you crazy fuck!" Because the masthead level was *138 feet* above the deck. If my timing was off by a nanosecond, within about two hours I'd be nothing but shark shit on the bottom of the ocean. "Please hold your questions until later," I said. "In the event of my demise, please hold your questions until we're all together again in hell." Then I jumped.

I'd already arranged with a buddy to film my stunt, because it was a Navy first. Even today, listening to his comments on the tape is still hilarious.

By the time I'd plummeted about 24,000 feet, he's growling, "Open the chute, now, damnit. C'mon! *Open* the son of a bitch, Marcinko!" Then, as I continued to drop like a cannonball, he's saying, "Goddamn you, Marcinko, you fucking hot-dog, *deploy*, goddamnit, *deploy!*" Then he gets into some *serious* profanity. Finally, as the camera captures my streaking body and the surface of the water *in the same frame*, he just moans. At that moment, I was dead even with the top of the masthead.

Then, *plap!* My chute flares open. I jerk upward. And I knife into the water.

The ship's skipper didn't even wait for me to come aboard before he started chewing me out. He began it over a bullhorn, and kept it up as I detached from my harness and swam to a skiff.

But the men jumping after me got the point: *do as I do*. They all executed fine HALO jumps themselves. And after that, none of them would ever have any problems taking orders from me.

I wasn't just a boss. I was a leader.

The Rogue Warrior Mentality: Lessons from Business

In 1987 several regions of the Domino's Pizza Incorporated chain were starting to flounder. Domino's had just slipped to second place in national taste-test surveys, and Pizza Hut, Domino's chief competitor, had just begun to deliver pizza—much to Domino's surprise and horror.

One of the regions that needed help most was the eastern region, centered in Baltimore.

Then a young corporate tiger named Kevin Williams took over that region. Williams had a bold plan. He wanted to put much more emphasis on the corporate stores, which the company directly owned, and less on the franchise stores. The corporate stores should have been cash cows, because they didn't have a franchise owner taking most of the profits. But the corporate stores were bleeding cash, apparently because their managers, who didn't *own* them, weren't very motivated. Williams had to change their attitudes, and do it fast. He desperately needed to inspire his troops.

So Williams started a blitzkrieg operation, going from corporate store to corporate store, and doing *whatever it took* to make each store work. Williams knew enough about the business to be able to quickly identify the weak spots in each store—but he didn't just *inform* the managers of their problems, and then move on. If a store needed more help baking pizzas, Williams stood at the ovens himself until the manager could find someone to fill that hole. If the store had a cashier who couldn't operate the register, Williams worked the register until the cashier caught on. If the floor needed sweeping, Williams swept it. He sent out a powerful message: No job is unimportant, *every* job has to be done right, and *everybody* is responsible for *everything*.

Williams's style was infectious. After he left a store, each employee in that store saw his or her job in a different light. If their job was important enough for a regional manager to do, then it was important enough for them to do—and do well! The managers, in particular, "saw the light." They realized that they were *just part of the team*, and that their job was to *help* their employees and not just to order them around.

Williams carried this same Rogue Warrior mentality to the regional corporate headquarters. He spent nights and weekends at work in a tireless effort to shut off the flow of red ink and revitalize company morale. Williams constantly preached personal responsibility to everyone at HQ. He insisted that his people think of themselves not in terms of their own limited job descriptions, but as troops in the service of the whole company.

With Williams leading the way so visibly, it didn't take long for the new attitude to catch on.

One incident clearly showed how values in Williams's region had begun to change.

Early one evening, a janitor at HQ was virtually the only person in the building when an office phone rang. It wasn't in the janitor's job description to answer the phone, but he did it anyway.

A corporate store manager in the region—a guy Williams had already inspired—was calling. He sounded frantic. He was almost out of cheese, and if he ran out, he'd have to close his store for the night, and lose thousands of dollars in sales. His store had been teetering on the brink of insolvency, and this might push it over.

The janitor didn't wait for an executive to tell him what to do. He rifled through desk drawers in the shipping office until he found a spare key to a truck. Then he commandeered the truck, drove to a supply house, and ordered some cheese—without having the authority to do so. Then he drove well over a hundred miles to deliver the cheese to the store.

He got there just as the store was running out of the last of its cheese.

The store stayed open.

Then the janitor drove back to HQ, but didn't have enough time left to do his regular job.

Williams heard about the incident the next day. He was delighted. He knew his style of "leading by helping" was paying off.

During Williams's tenure in that region, the number of Domino's outlets doubled and gross revenues soared. The crisis ended.

Kevin Williams, though, is just one example of a successful leader who asks his people to do only what he's willing to do first. Here are others:

- The leader of textile giant Milliken and Company, Roger Milliken—who's in his seventies—spends an estimated *one-third* of his time on his production floor. Often as not, he's on his *hands and knees*, examining the machinery that is the backbone of his operation. Furthermore, Milliken spends about 150 days each year out in the field, *literally* keeping his hands on his business.

• The director of the huge Nissan plant in Smyrna, Tennessee, wears the same coveralls to work that are worn by all of his production workers. Even when corporate big shots from Japan show up at the plant, he still sticks to his coveralls.

• Wayne Huizenga, the owner of a multibillion-dollar sports, entertainment, and waste-management empire, got his start in the garbage business—and he *still* rides garbage-truck routes when he's considering buying another waste-management company. Huizenga refuses to make decisions based solely on spreadsheets and corporate meetings. If he can't get in a truck, ride the routes, and spend his days talking to the garbage collectors, he won't make a deal.

Does Huizenga do this because he's nostalgic about the good old days, when he *had* to ride the trucks? Hell, no. He does it because he knows that to *understand* a business, you've got to stay *close* to the business.

And to be successful, you've got to truly *lead* the business. Not from the top down. But from the bottom up.

CHAPTER FOUR

THE FOURTH COMMANDMENT

"I shall punish thy bodies because the more thou sweatest in training, the less thou bleedest in combat."

The troops should be exercised frequently, cavalry as well as infantry, and the general should often be present to praise some, to criticize others, and to see with his own eyes that the orders are observed exactly.
—Frederick the Great

Training is all-encompassing and should be related to everything a unit does, or can have happen to it.
—Lieutenant General Arthur S. Collins, Jr.

It is a doctrine of war not to assume the enemy will not come, but rather to rely on one's readiness to meet him; not to presume that he will not attack, but rather to make one's self invincible.
—Sun Tzu, *The Art of War*

Whatever does not break my back makes me stronger.
—Friedrich Nietzsche

The man who spends more sleepless nights with his army, and who works harder in drilling his troops, runs the fewer risks in fighting the foe.
—The Emperor Maurice, *The Strategikon*

You know that phrase, "Your employees are your greatest asset"? It's bullshit.

Here's the truth: "Your *well-trained* employees are your greatest asset." The rest of them are just cannon fodder. Worse than that, they're the dumb sons of bitches that are going to screw up your mission and get *everybody* in deep shit.

I'll tell you what the difference was between my legendary SEAL Team Six and other famed special warfare teams, like the Army Rangers. The difference was, the Rangers would go out and kill some of the most bloodthirsty terrorists on earth—while SEAL Team Six would go out, make a high-altitude jump, then parasail ten miles *before* deploying their chutes, then swim ten miles, and *then* kill some of the most bloodthirsty terrorists on earth.

How did I prepare my men for that kind of feat? Simple. By training them so god-awful hard that by the time the mission rolled around, they were *relieved* that all they had to do was jump, parasail, swim, and then kill people. That kind of day at the office beat the *hell* out of another day of my training regimen.

If you train people properly, they won't be able to tell a drill from the real thing. If anything, the real thing will be *easier*.

I like to occasionally read psychology books, and I've discovered that it's currently in vogue to say that a lot of neurotic people are "compulsively self-reliant." The theory goes: Whenever you don't nurture a little kid enough and take care of his needs for him, he starts fending for himself at too early an age, and it screws him up. Because he's just a vulnerable little kid, with no real skills or power, he overcompensates with self-reliant overkill. Then, when he grows up, he keeps up this pattern, and is always paranoid about having enough backup systems and fail-safe devices. He can't relax until he's dotted every *i* and crossed every *t*. He makes his life miserable.

Well, I say, *find* that miserable son of a bitch and *hire* him—because that's exactly the type of guy you want beside you in the battles of business.

If you want to be with somebody who's laid-back and mellow, then go find Barney the fucking Dinosaur. But don't take him into *battle*; take him out to play golf, or drink beer, or to sing "I-love-you, you-love-me."

The more I work with major corporations, the clearer it is to me that, in most cases, the CEOs don't demand the preparedness and toughness from their people that the modern global environment demands. And then they wonder why the Japanese or the Koreans are kicking their asses around the block.

For example, most corporations spend a great deal of money, energy, and time developing strategic plans and tactics. But then they spend very little time "walking through" these plans—playing "war games," to see if the plans will actually *work* or if they'll just fall to pieces during the first visit from Mr. Murphy. I've been to dozens of executive seminars where the top officers make *detailed* battle plans. But then . . . that's it, the end. Golf time!

Instead, they ought to leave their goddamn golf clubs at home and do their "bonding" by war-gaming a real-life, real-time scenario, where they put their plan to the test. They ought to "play the enemy," and try to throw as many variables as possible at the plan. That will not only test their plan, but it will also give them an education in *how the enemy thinks*.

Red Cell, our team that tested the security of Navy installations by "playing terrorist," was extremely success-ful at uncovering vulnerabilities. We were allowed to think, act, and live like terrorists. And once we got into that mind-set, it was astonishingly easy to identify weak spots and exploit them. We could "see" the Navy better than it could see itself.

Do you know how your competition sees *you*?

If you'd done enough training, you *would*.

The Rogue Warrior Mentality: Lessons from War

When you're in war, you have to be ready to die. I don't mean ready to die just when you're in battle. I mean *all* the time—even when you're just training.

The fact is, if you're not training hard enough to risk death, you're not really training. You're just going through the motions. And if you're just going through the motions, you'll *never* be prepared for the real deal. When the real deal happens, I guarantee you, you're going to be *scared*. You're going to be *confused*. You're going to be worrying about your buddies. You're going to be dealing with Murphy. If, in your training, you haven't *already faced all these things*, you won't be prepared. When the real deal goes down, you won't know whether to shit or go blind.

And if that happens, you're not going to get a second chance. You're going to simply have the honor of dying for your country—when, as General Patton noted, it's a much better idea to let the other poor son of a bitch die for *his*.

I used to take SEAL Six out in the desert to practice High Altitude High Opening parachute jumps. The point of a HAHO jump is to bail out so far from your enemy that he'll never hear your plane. You may be twenty miles away when you jump. Then you use your chute as a parasail to quietly zero in on your target. By the time you finally arrive, the only way your enemy will know you're in his area is that when he looks down at his ass he'll find it's suddenly full of bullets.

But my men *hated* doing these jumps. Anybody in their right mind would have hated them. You got cold as hell, and you didn't even have enough air to breathe at the higher altitudes—you had to carry a "bail-out bottle" of oxygen for the early part of the fall. Plus, the jumps were dangerous—especially when you did about fifty of them. With that kind of frequency, the odds against you built up, and so did the chance that Sir Murphy would stop by to rape and pillage.

But I welcomed the danger, because I wanted my men to learn how to operate efficiently under stress. They had to be ready for *anything*, because, in combat, that's exactly what they'd get: enemy fire, failed chutes, tangled lines, broken bones on impact, etc.

The men realized this, but that didn't keep them from bitching about it. Didn't bother me. It was my job to punish their bodies and their job to piss and moan about it.

One night, in the moonlit desert, we made a jump so high that the lights from two towns a hundred miles apart merged into one little dot below us.

Shortly after we bailed out, I knew we had a problem. A hell of a problem—the kind you have nightmares about. The chute of one of the men, an experienced jumper named Simpson, didn't open. But Simpson reacted just as he'd been trained to react. He didn't panic. He cut away

6 3

his bad chute and let himself free-fall another couple of thousand feet, to make sure he was far away from the malfunctioning chute. Then he deployed his backup chute.

It didn't open. Murphy's goddamn Law.

We watched helplessly as he fell to his death.

To make matters more demoralizing, civilians recovered his body, and we had to go kidnap his broken remains from the morgue—because our operation was clandestine.

Next day, we were back in the air.

Nobody complained about the immediate resumption of training. Everyone understood. When you're a warrior, death is always looking over your shoulder.

And we all knew there was just one way to improve our odds of survival: train, train, train.

Sometimes, if your training is *properly intense*—it will kill you. More often—much, *much* more often—it will save your life.

The Rogue Warrior Mentality: Lessons from Business

Bill Bowerman was one of the great coaches, and great motivators, of the modern era of college sports. While he was track coach at the University of Oregon in the 1960s, he almost single-handedly created the jogging craze in America, by writing a best-seller about it and tirelessly promoting the concept. He won four national championships, coached twenty-eight Olympians, and coached the Olympic track team of 1972.

Bowerman was a *bear* on the subject of training. There was no such thing as a "good" reason to miss one of his track practices. His practices were tough and long, and he made his men train twelve months a year.

Moreover, he was a rabid believer in the concept of the student-athlete, and demanded that his runners excel academically.

Of course, it was hard as hell for his kids to be world-class athletes and also successful students. Sometimes his runners bitched about Bowerman's expectations, but Bowerman never showed any sympathy for their weakness. If you wanted to be on one of Bowerman's national championship teams, you had to run *and* study. Bowerman's constant demand was, don't whine about training, just do it, because it's the only way to be a winner. On his teams, there was only one way of doing things, and that was the *Bowerman* way.

His men didn't consider Bowerman a tyrant, though, because he was out there with them, every day. If *they* had a problem, *he* had a problem. Bowerman was a true Servant Leader.

One of Bowerman's star student-athletes was a kid named "Buck" Knight, and Bowerman rode him particularly hard, because Knight had a great deal of promise as an athlete and as a student.

Knight liked to play as hard as he worked, and sometimes he'd procrastinate about studying for his exams. When that would happen, Bowerman would chew out

Knight's ass and tell him, "If you have to stay up all night studying, just do it and don't bitch about it—but *don't miss practice.*" He told Knight that if he missed one practice, he'd get a warning—and if he missed two, he was off the team. To Bowerman, training was more than even an ethic. It was a way of life.

Knight learned his values from Bowerman: Plan for every eventuality, take nothing for granted, enter every competition stronger than your competitor, *expect* things to go wrong, and have a backup plan for when they do.

Knight graduated and went into business. He became only moderately successful, but didn't give up. He kept looking for new opportunities and kept studying new ways to start a small business. Bowerman had told him that a person's *real* education comes *after* college, in the real world, and Knight took the lesson to heart.

Around 1970 Bowerman started experimenting with ways to get more bounce out of track shoes. He abandoned the standard flat soles with sharp cleats and tried to design a rubber sole with punched-out crevices. He finally came up with a workable prototype for a sole by pouring hot plastic into his wife's waffle iron—creating a "waffle sole."

Bowerman and Knight began working together, trying to market the waffle-soled shoes. The shoes became popular. Phil "Buck" Knight called them Nikes and sold them out of a storefront in Eugene, Oregon, where he'd trained under Bowerman.

Nike expanded rapidly, partly because of Knight's insistence on balls-to-the-wall training. His sales force, in particular, was the best trained in the industry, and they prepared for every eventuality. When the jogging craze dropped off in the 1980s, Nike was totally prepared. They shifted their emphasis to other sports, and to sportswear, and emerged stronger than ever.

By the 1990s Bill Bowerman was a multimillionaire from his Nike stock. Buck Knight was one of the richest men in America and probably the most powerful man in the world of sports.

Knight—now a full-fledged Rogue Warrior—had moved his operation to Portland, and had built an immense campus of office buildings to house Nike's world headquarters. To enter the Nike campus, all visitors now drive down a street called One Bowerman Way.

Phil Knight is a notable example of a leader who built an industry-dominating company from scratch by emphasizing training; IBM founder Tom Watson, Sr., is another.

Training, more than any other single element, is what turned IBM into a $7.5 billion company. In the earliest days of IBM, Watson had only one person on his staff: a director of education.

That may sound like an extreme emphasis on training, but consider this:

- At IBM, it's not uncommon to undergo *significant* retraining every three years.
- Every IBM employee who gets a promotion is *automatically* placed in a training program.
- At IBM, all executives must spend at least forty hours a year in classroom training.

Just a few years ago, it looked as if Apple were going to

knock IBM off its pedestal. As recently as 1993, IBM was losing money. Apple was "new" and "young." Apple was "the future." But IBM didn't pull into a shell—it aggressively retooled and retrained. Apple, however, got complacent. Now it's Apple that looks old and IBM that looks futuristic. In its second fiscal quarter of 1996 alone, Apple lost more than $69 million. IBM, however, is thriving.

When you train and train and *retrain*, you don't just control the present. You learn to *adapt*—and control the *future*.

CHAPTER FIVE

THE FIFTH
COMMANDMENT

"Indeed, if thou hurteth in thy efforts and thou suffer painful dings, then thou art Doing It Right."

Pressure is a word that is misused in our vocabulary. When you start thinking of pressure, it's because you've started to think of failure.
   —Tommy Lasorda, manager of the Los Angeles Dodgers

A man's reach should exceed his grasp, or what's a heaven for?
                                                    —Robert Browning

We must go on and on, until we drop.
                                                    —Winston Churchill

Too many leaders today confuse efficiency with ease. They think that if they've found the easiest way to do something, they've found the most efficient way. But they're stupid as *hell* to believe this. The only reason they *do* believe it is that they *want* to believe it.

Efficiency means doing something *fast and well.* Ease means doing it in a way that *doesn't hurt.*

71

But if the job you're doing doesn't hurt, you're *fucking up!* You're not being efficient; you're just being soft and lazy. You're looking for the path of least resistance—and, believe me, that path is only for *losers.*

Over the last fifty years, America has been engulfed by institutionalism. These days, practically everything is a big, bureaucratic institution: business, labor, education, health care, media—you name it. And one of the worst things that has come from this institutionalism is the loss of *personal willingness to feel pain.*

Because we're all surrounded by institutions, we no longer feel that we should *have* to suffer. Suffering is now seen as an unfortunate, temporary aberration, or even as a "disease." We think we should be insulated from pain by insurance, or by government aid, or by a support group, or by some drug like Prozac. At the very least, we think we should be able to dump our problems in the laps of our employers.

But in this country, it wasn't always like that. In earlier, tougher days, when people depended upon *themselves* to solve their own problems, people didn't run from difficulty and discomfort like scared sheep. They endured suffering bravely, and *used* it, to gain strength. Battle scars were worn with pride. As a nation, and as a culture, we endorsed Nietzsche's dictum, "Whatever does not break my back makes me stronger."

We saw difficulty as a *challenge*—not as a *threat.*

Currently, though, when a manager demands that his subordinates work so hard that they actually *hurt*, the manager is branded as a tyrant or a sadist. The union files

a grievance against him, and his company demotes him—
or fires him.

These days, when you ask employees to make a *sacrifice*,
they think it means giving up part of their *dental plan*.

In war, my men invariably bitched when I pushed them
so hard it hurt, but they always understood that pain was
good for them. They were serious men on serious missions, and they recognized that pain was nothing more
than just another communication signal. Pain was their
body's way of telling them that they'd pushed themselves
to their limits—which was exactly where they were
supposed to be. If they were operating at the height of their
limits, they were doing everything they could to fulfill the
number one rule of being a soldier: At the end of your
mission, go home alive.

If *you*, in your work, are not pushing yourself to your
limits every *day*, then you're just another salary-stealing
punk who's tagging after the *real* men.

So many benefits come from pain.

One clear benefit is that people who learn to endure
pain learn about *themselves*. They learn their limitations,
they learn the full extent of their abilities, and they learn
how to motivate themselves.

Also, the people on your team who learn to endure pain
will become, quite rightfully, *proud* of themselves. And
they'll also become proud of the other team members.
They will develop self-respect and respect for the team.
Thus, you will establish a powerful sense of esprit de
corps.

You will develop team members who will be loyal to

each other. When one team member sees another one hurting—for the good of the team—he'll do whatever he can to help.

In the business world, pain is usually more mental than physical. Mental exhaustion should be so common in your office that, by the end of the day, people will be walking around with blank stares. They should be bumping into walls. If they're not beat to hell by sundown, you're being too easy on them—and you're setting yourself up for defeat.

Think that's *harsh?* It *is.* But do you think that the manager in Japan or Korea or Mexico who wants *to steal your business* isn't harsh? Think again. He *is.* If you really want to *protect* your people, push them. Hard.

Even more common in business than mental pain, though, is psychological pain. Many men who can endure the intellectual pain of extended rigorous thinking fall apart when they're confronted with psychological pain. Sometimes this psychological pain comes from the loneliness of being separated from their families by frequent business trips. Other times, the psychological pain comes from the fear of failure.

But the most *constant source* of psychological pain in business is simply *change.* Change hurts. It makes people insecure, confused, and angry. People want things to be the same as they've always been, because that makes life easier. But if you're a leader, you can't let your people hang on to the past.

Often, people are passive-aggressive about change, pretending to embrace it, while secretly sabotaging it. Get *rid* of these people. They're jeopardizing everyone else on the team.

Be wary when one of your people tells you that a change you've instituted "isn't working." In reality, it may be working *fine*—but simply causing pain.

Likely as not, when your people tell you a change "isn't working," they won't even know they're lying to you. They'll be so addicted to the concept of institutional protection from pain that they won't even see that *some good things have to hurt.* They'll just assume that if something hurts, there *must* be a better way to do it.

It will be up to you, as the leader, to remind them that there's a difference between efficiency and ease.

And it will be up to you—leading from the front—to show them that the *hard* way, the way that *hurts*, is usually the *best* way.

The Rogue Warrior Mentality: Lessons from War

Jim "Patches" Watson, the point man for my platoon in Vietnam, sagged to the ground and exhaled. "Minefield up ahead, boss," he said.

He'd spotted the button detonator of a VC mine. It was an antipersonnel mine—the type that is just powerful enough to blow off your legs and balls, but otherwise do no serious damage.

"You up to it?" I asked him. I meant, was he up to leading the platoon through the minefield from the point position?

"No prob," he said. But I didn't buy it. He looked

wasted. His eyes were full of red veins, his uniform was slick with sweat, and his breathing was shallow and mechanical. He'd taken the point all day long, and now, at nightfall, he had nothing left to give.

"I'll take us in," I told Patches. He started to protest, but I cut him off.

This was early in my first tour, and I didn't have much experience with walking point yet, so I asked Patches to tell me some of the tricks of the trade. He filled me in on a lot of technical stuff about what to watch for and listen for.

When he finished, I asked, "How'll I know if I'm doin' it right?"

"You'll know you're doin' it right," he said, "when everything hurts."

"Everything?"

He nodded and pointed at his eyes, his neck, his back, his feet, his hands, even his ears. "*All* of it," he said.

We headed out. The entire platoon was strung out behind me in a path no more than a foot wide. We inched along in silence.

I scanned the ground in front of me intensely. Every bump was a threat. I listened to the surrounding countryside so hard that I could hear the blood circulating in my own ears. I sniffed the air for any revealing odors. I walked all hunched over, but didn't make a sound.

After thirty minutes, my shirt was glued to my body with sweat. My eyes burned. My ears were so "open" that every time a bird screeched, I damn near jumped out of my boots.

An hour later, I straightened up and heard bones pop in my spine. I allowed my attention to shift to my own body and was suddenly aware that every muscle ached and that my senses were so on edge that it hurt just to look and listen.

Now I knew what Patches meant. Everything hurt. All of it. It meant I was doing a good job.

I welcomed the pain. I welcomed it on behalf of myself, my men, my wife, my children, my testicles, and the United States Navy. I was happy to have that pain. It was my buddy.

We kept moving, no more than a few feet a minute. I began to sense something. I can't say I *heard* anything, or *saw* anything, or *felt* anything, or *smelled* anything. But all of my senses, working together, suddenly said, Danger!

I rasped, "Down! Now!" and everyone hit the deck.

As I dropped, the blast of an AK-47 singed the back of my neck. The VC were *ten feet* from us, in the bush.

We hit them with a volley so compressed that it came at them like a wall and knocked them back. Then one of my men rose to his knees and blazed away with an antitank weapon. *BAMM!* Some of the VC were thrown into the air, and the others screamed and burrowed into the dirt.

I waved my hand in a circle. "Clear *out!*" I yelled.

We charged back down the trail we'd cleared. Within a few minutes, we were safe—or, as safe as you ever got in the jungles of Vietnam.

When we finally got back to our barracks, Patches bought me a beer. Then I bought him one.

I'd faced another battle, and I'd learned another lesson: When all you want to do is *win,* you don't *mind* pain.

At the point of ultimate challenge, pain is your best friend. It tells you you're doing it right.

77

The Rogue Warrior Mentality: Lessons from Business

One of the heroes of World War II's Normandy invasion, and of the Battle of the Bulge, was a young American enlisted man named Phil Weltman. Weltman started these campaigns as a private first class. But during the battles, he rose to the rank of top sergeant, and finally received a rare battlefield commission, as a lieutenant, advancing to that rank as the men above him were all killed. He was also awarded the French Croix de Guerre.

Weltman could easily have avoided battle, because he was a leading agent in the world's most prominent talent agency, the William Morris Company. Weltman could have used his high-level connections to stay out of combat. For example, shortly before the Battle of the Bulge, Weltman had had breakfast with touring USO star Dinah Shore, who was one of his clients, and with General George S. Patton. But Weltman never considered pulling strings to stay safe. It would have violated his code of personal responsibility.

In the Army, Weltman learned a set of leadership principles. These principles inspired his men to be fiercely loyal and tremendously effective. After the war, he applied these principles to business and became one of the more powerful people in Hollywood. He also became a mentor to many rising young men in the entertainment industry.

One of the principles he learned was, "You don't *seek* leadership. You *have* leadership." He also learned the concept of "leading by helping." He learned to hate bureaucracy, and taught his subordinates to keep their systems streamlined, small, and simple. He learned how to chew men out, and then forget his anger and move on. And he learned that, often as not, there was no *easy way* to achieve a hard goal—and that only losers shied away from pain.

At the William Morris office after the war, Weltman started each day with a quick meeting. At 9 sharp, he'd slap his hand on the table and bark, "Let's get this show on the road!" If anyone was late, they missed out—no repetition, no recap. Once, a young agent missed the entire meeting. Weltman asked the guy's secretary where he was, and she gave him the agent's home number.

Weltman called. "What are you doing at *home?*"

"I'm so buried in scripts, I stayed home to get through them. Easier that way."

"You're through," said Weltman. "Come clean out your desk. But wait until the weekend."

"Why?"

"I'll be gone. That'll make it *easier* on you."

Another time, Weltman found one of his young agents reading a newspaper on the job. Fired him—on the spot.

Weltman was tough as hell, and subordinates didn't last long around him if they followed the path of least resistance. But many of his young charges were on fire with ambition and were more than willing to accept a little pain.

One of the kids Weltman trained was Bob Shapiro, who later became president of Warner Brothers. Another youngster was Joe Wizan, who became head of Twentieth Century Fox. Another was Barry Diller, who later ran

Paramount, and ran Fox, and who created the Fox television network.

And another Weltman protégé was Michael Ovitz, who later became the most powerful man in modern Hollywood, as the president of Creative Artists Agency.

Still another was an ambitious young kid named Ron Meyer, whom Weltman considered "the son I never had."

Ron Meyer tried as hard as anyone to follow Weltman's rules, no matter how painful they were. He worked from seven A.M. until seven P.M., six days a week, at a furious pace. The schedule *hurt*—mentally, physically, and psychologically—but Weltman thought it was making a man out of Meyer.

One Friday afternoon, though, Meyer couldn't take it any longer, and instead of going to lunch, he drove to a friend's house in Palm Springs, for a long weekend.

Somehow, Weltman found out.

Weltman was in genuine pain, because he hated the idea of firing his "son." But he wouldn't tolerate weakness. If Meyer couldn't take it, he was out.

Weltman called Meyer's secretary and told her he wanted Meyer in his office in two hours, at 4:30. There was no way Meyer could get back in time. And if Meyer didn't show—*on time*—Weltman would fire him.

Weltman felt almost physically ill.

When Meyer got the message from his secretary, he was out by the pool in Palm Springs, dripping wet.

Weltman stared at the clock on his wall as the afternoon ticked by. At 4:30, Weltman swallowed hard.

All of a sudden, Ron Meyer burst into the room, freshly shaved, with a suit on.

He had changed clothes and shaved in the car. At 110 mph.

Weltman was tremendously relieved. Meyer had skirted the rules, but he'd made it to the meeting on time—the *hard* way.

Weltman never mentioned Palm Springs—and Meyer didn't either.

Several years later, when Phil Weltman reached age sixty-five, he was unceremoniously retired from the William Morris Company. In protest, Mike Ovitz, Ron Meyer, and three other agents left Morris and started Creative Artists Agency.

Ovitz and Meyer became the two most powerful men in the motion picture business. They deliberately patterned the CAA business ethic after the principles that Phil Weltman had learned in war. In the lobby of the CAA office was one portrait, of Phil Weltman.

In 1995 Ovitz left CAA to become president of Disney.

The same year, Ron Meyer became president of the immense entertainment conglomerate MCA.

There was some irony, of course, in the two former partners—and former protégés of "Rogue Warrior" Phil Weltman—becoming rivals.

But neither had accepted his new job because it looked *easy*. In fact, they'd taken the new jobs mostly for the *challenge*.

They'd learned a valuable lesson from Phil Weltman: The path of least resistance is the path of the loser.

Good things usually hurt.

CHAPTER SIX

THE SIXTH COMMANDMENT

*"Thou hast not to like it—
thou hast just to do it."*

Well done is better than well said.
                              —Benjamin Franklin

Knowing how to handle pressure is necessary for survival.
                              —Admiral James Stockdale

The Buddha said the first lesson that everyone must learn is that "life is sorrow."

If you are a warrior, you understand how true this is. You understand it because, throughout your life, you have done things you *did not want to do*. You have accomplished some missions that were painful and others that were excruciating.

But you *accepted* pain, because your focus was solely on accomplishing your mission. You never stopped to even *think* about whether or not you *liked* these painful missions.

You knew that if you did only what you *wanted* to do, you would be missing out on *life itself*: because life is part pain, and part pleasure, and the man who tries to live only the "good" parts of life is the man who ends up *not living at all.*

If you are a warrior who has lived life to the fullest, accepting both pleasure and pain, then you're probably ready for leadership. If, in your battles, you've learned to *welcome* a tough challenge, you probably already have a strong sense of personal responsibility and duty. In short, you already have *character.* And if you have character, you're ready for command. All you need is the opportunity.

If your subordinates see that you are willing to do things that you *hate* to do, they will be willing to do things *they* hate. Like you, they'll accept pain for the good of the team.

General William Tecumseh Sherman, often called "the first modern general," made a point of riding in muddy ditches beside his columns of troops, to avoid forcing his men off the road. It was one way he could show them that he was willing to suffer along with them, and make their lives a little easier.

When Admiral James Stockdale flew missions in the skies above Vietnam, he obviously accepted the painful fact that he might be killed or captured. When he *was* captured, he made the difficult decision to be a model prisoner of war, even though this would subject him to torture and privation.

At one low point in his brutal captivity, Stockdale—who later became a candidate for vice president of the United States—feared that if he was tortured any further, he would give up military secrets. Therefore, to negate that possibility, Stockdale beat himself unconscious with a stool in his cell.

Stockdale was a true leader. He didn't always like his mission. But he had learned to totally disregard his own personal desires. They were irrelevant.

I learned this from him firsthand, when I worked for him in the Pentagon on my first staff tour in Washington, D.C. He offered constant guidance, by word and action.

To him, only one thing mattered: *accomplishing the mission.*

The Rogue Warrior Mentality: Lessons from War

It wouldn't be *normal* for men to *like* a training regimen of deep-water diving, high-altitude parachuting, demolition missions, and long-distance swimming. And, God knows, my men—as exceptional as they were—were quite normal about having to endure hardship. They *hated* the shit that I put them through during our long months of "saturation training."

The intent of saturation training—intense, repetitive, hyper-training—is to simulate the conditions of war. For example, as part of their training exercise, my men were required by the Navy to do one high-altitude parachute jump every quarter year. But I made them do *fifty jumps.* That way, they ended up feeling just as they would in a battle: exhausted, angry, confused, and scared.

One evening, in the middle of our saturation training regimen, SEAL Team Six pulled into Eglin Air Force Base, in Florida. The men were already drained and bruised, but some of the toughest training was still ahead.

For starters, we had to greet the dawn from the belly of a modified Boeing 727, then drop six miles through the air, land in the ocean, deploy an inflatable boat, and make our way to shore.

No one wanted to do it. Not me. Not anybody. The guy who especially didn't want to do it was my old swim buddy from Underwater Demolition Team training, a master chief named Mac, who didn't even like *heights*— let alone, *jumping* from them. But Mac was a vital part of our unit, because he was experienced, smart, and as brave as they come. He was my senior enlisted man and my top adviser on the morale of the team. When Mac's morale was low, *everybody's* was, because all the young guys looked up to him.

Mac's morale was definitely down the night we dragged ass into Eglin. He was dreading that first long step out of the plane in the morning.

Mac slipped into the base's noncommissioned officers' club to pound down enough beer to happily face the day ahead. And that's where I found him, parked at the bar, sitting next to an old-timer from World War II who was attending a bomber squadron reunion—I think it was the

407th, which I believe was the group that beat the shit out of General Rommel in North Africa.

The old soldier's name was Vern, and he was knocking back Budweisers so efficiently as he reminisced about the war that Mac and I had to apply ourselves diligently to keep up.

He began telling us about *his* training missions during the Big War. Before he'd shipped out for Africa, he'd been stationed in Idaho, where he'd been the flight chief for James Stewart, the actor, who had enlisted in the Air Force as a pilot.

Stewart, the old soldier said, was an aw-shucks kind of guy on the ground, but once he got in the air, he was an *animal*, the kind of pilot who liked to do things like *fly through* an empty hangar every morning, just to get his heart started.

One day, the old sergeant said, he and Stewart were out on a training run in the Sawtooth Mountain Range, when one of their primary navigation instruments screwed up. In a matter of minutes, they were completely lost. They were low on fuel and were starting to think about bringing the plane down—*anywhere*. But then they crossed over a mountain crest, and after that they couldn't find any place flat enough to land. Crossing the crest had sucked up most of the fuel they had left. Now they *really needed* to land—so, of course, they couldn't. It was the 1940s' corollary of Murphy's Law: Murphy's *Grandfather's* Law.

They picked their way through a maze of peaks and cliffs, as their fuel dwindled.

Stewart, the sarge said, didn't know *what* the hell to do. So, like a *smart* leader, who respects his fellow warriors,

89

he asked for help. "Stewart told me, 'Wall, ah . . . Varn . . . ah, if you got any . . . *ideas* . . . I'm *listenin'*.'"

The sergeant took over. He knew a bunch of navigating tricks, and he knew how to stay calm in a bad situation. He'd grown up in Dodge City at the end of the cowboy days, and he was tough enough to bite the head off a rattlesnake and resourceful enough to farm wheat in the Dust Bowl. He was, in short, a leader waiting for the opportunity to lead.

He led them back to the crest that had locked them into the mountains. "I told Stewart, 'This is *it*—If we don't get back over that ridge, we ain't *gettin'* back.'"

But they couldn't get a run at the crest that was long enough to get them the altitude they'd need to vault over the top.

"So Stewart says, 'Wall, ah, I guess, ah, we're just gonna have to kinda . . . *corkscrew* . . . us some altitude.'" So Stewart started flying in an upward spiral, repeatedly banking away from the crest just before they crashed into it.

Finally, they took one last swing at the mountain. The snowy peak rushed at them. They skipped over the top.

I wanted to know if the old soldier had been sitting off to the side on that last run, checking instruments, or if he'd been sitting up front, where he could see all the gory details. So I asked, "Where were you *sitting* on that last run?"

He gave me a blank look through his thick bifocals.

"Where was I *sitting*? Why, I was sitting in a *pile of shit*, of course!" he said.

Mac slapped him on the back.

I bought him another Budweiser. "But I bet you were right back at it the next day—huh?" I said.

"Hell, yes, we were back at it. That was the *job*. I hated that goddamn job. But, you know, it was *war*. You just *did* it. Besides, it was still better than tryin' to paint barns in a dust storm."

"Why'd you try to *paint* in a dust storm?" Mac asked.

"*Had* to. The storm *lasted* six *years*. It was the *Dust Bowl*."

He told us a little bit about his life. He'd retired with $300,000 in the bank—after a career in a factory at $2.50 to $5.00 per hour. How? "Overtime," he said. Then, at age 70, he'd built his retirement home with his own hands. After that, he'd built a couple more houses, for his sons.

No doubt about it, the people in this guy's generation were tough sons of bitches. To them, after enduring the Depression, and then kicking Hitler's ass, making a living was like a *vacation*. If people *still* had that same toughness, this country would be even stronger than it is.

"But I'll tell you one thing I learned up there with Stewart that day," the old sergeant said. "When you're in a bad spot like that, you just keep your head and do your *job*. You do it until there's nuthin' else *to* do. Then, if you get the chance, *close your eyes*, cuz it beats the *hell* outta *seein'* what's gonna kill you."

Mac nodded. It was good advice.

About six hours later, at 0700, Mac and I were together again, staring out the slide of the 727 at the water far, far below. The other men had just left.

Mac looked bad. "Ladies first," I said. I punched his arm.

He took another look at the water—closed his eyes—and jumped. He obviously didn't want to jump. He just did it.

The Rogue Warrior Mentality: Lessons from Business

THUMP! THUMP! THUMP! A straggler beat on the outside of the door of the decrepit plane, causing the chickens in the aisle to cackle, but the crew, ready for takeoff, paid no attention.

Author Sidney Sheldon and actress Deborah Raffin, in Inner Mongolia to make a movie deal, sat transfixed, watching a man drop a live rat into a straw basket. Sheldon's wife, Jorja Cutright, had tears in her eyes. Raffin's husband, producer Michael Viner—the *organizer* of this expedition—held Jorja's hand and prayed.

Before the group had boarded, a crowd of Chinese had surrounded Raffin, clutching at her and chanting, "Nightmare! Nightmare!" What did *that* mean? Foreign *devil*? As the engines revved for takeoff, Viner explained to his wife that one of her more forgettable films, *Nightmare in Badham County*, had garnered *250 million* paid admissions in China (a nation that can't afford better-known American movies). Thus, she was an icon in China.

The film's gross, though, had been held down by the five-cent ticket price. The real money, Viner said, had come from the Chinese edition of her autobiography, which sold *eight million copies*. As a producer—the family's businessman—Viner had to know these things. He didn't like doing business this way. But business was business, so he just did it.

Inner Mongolia wasn't even as bad as their last stop had been. There, in the Philippines, corrupt officials had copied Viner's film during a customs inspection, and on his way to the movie's world premiere at the Manila Film Festival, he'd seen cassettes of it at a bazaar. At the festival, he'd been impressed with the special effects in one Philippine film, until he realized they'd been spliced out of Raiders of the Lost Ark. The footage had kept cutting between amazing special effects and Filipinos with bazookas.

Viner stood up—the plane had no seat belts—to see why the man had dropped the rat into his basket.

"He was feeding his snake," Viner later recalled.

Finally, just before they began to taxi, a flight attendant, sick of the thump-thump-thump, unlocked the door. A man jumped in. It was the pilot.

Jorja Cutright began to weep. Viner stared glumly out the window and wondered what the hell it would take for him to become a major success in Hollywood.

The plane shuddered down the runway. It hopped into the air. Then it smacked back down onto the runway. Again, it struggled upward. It climbed a hundred feet. It dropped. Viner held his breath. Just before it hit the ground, it straightened up and began to climb.

It maintained power and got safely aloft.

Viner finally exhaled, loosened the top button of his shirt, and sat back to relax—in a pile of shit, no doubt.

Within a few years, Michael Viner's willingness to endure tribulation had paid off. In addition to producing, he created the Dove Books on Tape company and became a major part of the meteoric rise of the audio-book industry. He willingly made sacrifices for Dove—as he had in other businesses—and Dove became a leader in the industry.

From that base of power, he began to publish hardcover books. In 1995, as one of the few prominent publishers based in Los Angeles, he was able to achieve spectacular success by publishing books about the O. J. Simpson trial.

Obviously, the competition to publish books about the Simpson trial was fierce. But that didn't stop Viner. He just dug in and *did* it.

After all, when things got tough, and Viner needed a break, he could still drift back nostalgically to his days as a "Rogue Warrior" in Inner Mongolia: *Ahhh!* . . . the *good* old days, when life was *sweet.*

CHAPTER SEVEN

THE SEVENTH COMMANDMENT

"Thou shalt Keep It Simple, Stupid."

The art of war is a simple art.

—Napoleon

In war, only what is simple can succeed.
—Field Marshal Paul von Hindenburg

Many of today's managers are in love with complicated systems. They think that if their systems are complex, then they must be *real smart sons of bitches* to be able to run them.

Of course, if they think this, they're actually dumb sons of bitches.

97

The more complex any system or strategy is, the more likely it will be to fail. Complex systems and strategies fail simply because they *are* complex—they have too many components, and the failure of any one component can screw up the entire operation. Also, they're hard for human beings to understand, so they greatly increase the chance of human error. In addition, they're hard to fix when they break. Lastly, they usually don't adapt well to changing situations.

All of these drawbacks make complex systems and strategies perilously dangerous.

If you are trying to manage a large, complex organization, you should not even *try* to adjust yourself to the organization. You should make the organization adjust to *you.*

One good way to do this is to break your organization into small teams. Each team should have no more than about ten members. Each team should have as much freedom as possible to do its own job in its own way. Each team should keep its own internal systems as simple as possible, and should concentrate on the basics.

When you run your company with small teams, you'll be able to respond quickly to crises and to immediately repair malfunctioning systems.

Another important way to achieve simplification is to create as streamlined a chain of command as possible. Everyone should have just one boss, if that's at all possible. And only the most vital issues should have to be approved by the men at the top of the chain. Give your people *authority.* If they abuse it, get rid of them.

In every possible way, you must constantly stress simplicity. You must demand it from your subordinates, and you've got to practice what you preach. Keep your instructions to your subordinates simple. Keep memos short. Insist on short reports from your managers. Don't speak in technocratic gobbledygook. Don't bog down in details. Make your people master the basics. Don't stray too far from your core business. Don't use more technology than you really need. Don't hire people permanently unless you *need* them permanently. Keep your chain of command as short as possible.

If you do all this, you'll have a company that will operate with simplicity and efficiency.

The Rogue Warrior Mentality: Lessons from War

On the night of April 24, 1980, I sat in a smoky war room of the Pentagon, looking at a series of huge communications screens, and at the worried faces of dozens of high-ranking military officials. We were all set to rescue our nation's hostages from Iran. But I had a sick feeling in my stomach.

Our plan was just too goddamn complicated.

We were going to take the hostages out of Iran in helicopters, but there were just too *many* choppers involved. Also, the chain of command was long and tangled. In the Pentagon were officers from all of the military services, and representatives from various federal agencies. And everybody thought *he* knew the best course of action.

Out in the field, we had chopper pilots who had focused

too much on the complexities of the plan, and not enough on the basics, like how to fly in the desert.

I had been part of the hostage-rescue task force from the beginning, and I'd fought hard to keep the rescue effort simple. But I had been overruled.

To me, it had looked like our biggest problem was the Iranian Air Force. Once we had pulled the hostages out of Tehran, we would be pursued by the Ayatollah's fighter pilots. We were planning to carry the hostages by helicopter to an airstrip about half an hour away from Tehran, then load them onto an evacuation cargo plane. But during the loading, we would be sitting ducks for the Iranian jets.

I had proposed that we bomb the runways at the Tehran airport, just before the hostages were rescued. That would prevent the Iranian planes from pursuing us.

I further recommended that we bomb the runways with bombs that were attached to parachutes and rigged to look like U.S. soldiers. These decoys would increase the diversionary element of the bombing raid. The Iranian military would be preoccupied with stopping an "invasion" by U.S. troops, which would divert its attention from our rescue attempt.

The Chairman of the Joint Chiefs of Staff, however, did not approve my raid on the airport. He thought that it might result in the death of civilians.

Instead, he recommended simply using more helicopters in the rescue. That way, if one was attacked or grounded, the others might be able to come save it. It was a typical institutional response: Just throw *more manpower, machinery, and money* at a problem, and hope for the best.

On the night of the raid, it didn't take long for the entire situation to become totally fucked up. First, two choppers flew into a sandstorm and got lost. Now we had to save not only the hostages, but also two rescue teams.

Then Murphy's goddamn Law shifted into overdrive. A bus with Iranian civilians drove by our staging site in the desert and couldn't help but notice this *horde* of American copters. We had to detain the bus. Now, what the hell did we do with fifty Iranian bus passengers? Shoot them? Call them fifty *cabs*?

Then a tanker truck drove by, and he naturally saw all the choppers and the bus. He made a run for it, so we fired on him, and suddenly we had a tanker sending smoke hundreds of feet into the air.

Then, during refueling, one of our aircraft hit another, and *BOOM!* We listened in painful helplessness as American servicemen were burned to death.

We got the survivors on the remaining helicopters and hauled ass for home.

The rescue effort had been planned for over six months. It had been *over*planned. It had been *over*staffed. It had depended too much on high-tech equipment.

It had been *anything but simple.*

And it had been one of the most miserable failures in American special warfare history.

Because I'm an optimist, I would like to think that the Joint Chiefs of Staff learned an important lesson that night: keep it simple, stupid.

I just wish they had learned that philosophy earlier— before it had cost all those lives.

101

The Rogue Warrior Mentality: Lessons from Business

In the early 1980s, the NBC television network was on the verge of going tits-up. It was bleeding money, it was getting mangled by its two chief rivals, CBS and ABC, and it didn't have a single hit show.

Then Grant Tinker took over. Tinker, who had been married to Mary Tyler Moore, had made a fortune running the MTM production company. At MTM, he'd had an extremely simple management style: He'd hired the best people and then let them do their jobs.

This had resulted in the production of popular, high-quality shows like *The Mary Tyler Moore Show, Lou Grant, WKRP in Cincinnati,* and *Hill Street Blues.*

At MTM, Tinker had been guided by more than just a desire to make himself rich. He fervently believed that American network television programming was awful, and that most of the network shows were "like human elimination—just *waste.*" Tinker, who was especially critical of his predecessor at NBC, schlockmeister Fred Silverman, said network programming was a "national crime" and "someone should go to jail for it . . . probably network executives."

Tinker was a true Rogue Warrior, and better programming was his cause.

Fred Silverman, in contrast to Tinker, *loved* lowbrow shows. He was also noted for his penchant for micromanagement and for the chaotic conditions he created. Under Silverman, the other executives at NBC had referred to

102

themselves as "the waiters." Silverman had typically dictated the contents of shows; had rushed them onto the air (at enormous expense); had chosen the actors, writers, and directors himself; and had made all the scheduling decisions. Net result: a last-place network.

When Tinker took over at NBC, he arranged the grand unveiling of his new master strategy. It took place at the annual meeting of the NBC local station managers. These people were the backbone of the network. If several of them were to jump ship and move to another network, it might kill the already moribund NBC.

The day of the managers' meeting was as festive as the network's promotions department could make it. The managers assembled in a huge auditorium in a Beverly Hills hotel. Music from a reggae band crashed around the room as a troupe of dancers, dressed in wild calypso costumes, bounded down the aisles. Women with a drizzle of glitter over their chests cavorted around a pink man on stilts.

Then a voice overrode the deafening music and began crying out the names of the NBC stars, as the actors paraded down the aisles. Ted Danson! Mr. T! Cybill Shepherd!

After the extravagant parade of stars, Grant Tinker mumbled, "I don't know whether to enlist or go have lunch."

Tinker took the podium. Then he announced the monumental strategy that was going to lead the network to the promised land.

"I'm going to get the best people," Tinker said, "and let them do good work."

The local managers waited expectantly. Yes—and what *else*? Anything? That's *it*?

The air of excitement hissed out of the room. Shoulders sagged. Station managers looked at one another as if to say, "What kind of . . . simple . . . bullshit *is* this?"

Shortly after, the season began. One of Tinker's first major decisions was to leave an abysmally rated show on the air, because he thought its producer was "good at his job." That show was *Cheers*. He also allowed an even *lower-ranked* show to survive because he thought its producer was "good at his job." That was *Family Ties*. He put on a hospital show that flopped miserably, but he stayed with the show because, as he said, he "liked it." That was *St. Elsewhere*. And then Tinker hired a very competent actor-producer and let him do the kind of show he wanted. That was Bill Cosby, and the result was *The Cosby Show*, the most successful TV program of the decade.

Within two years, NBC was the top-ranked network. Despite occasional setbacks, NBC has remained one of the strongest entertainment companies in the world.

Grant Tinker, deservedly, was given most of the credit for saving NBC. Program critics and business analysts called him a genius.

Tinker *was* a genius. He was smart enough to keep it simple.

Chapter Eight

THE EIGHTH COMMANDMENT

"Thou shalt never assume."

The practical measures that we take are always based on the assumption that our enemies are not unintelligent.
— Achidamus II, King of Sparta

An important difference between a military operation and a surgical operation is that the patient is not tied down. But it is a common fault of generalship to assume that he is.
— Captain Sir Basil Liddell Hart

I hope you have kept the enemy always in the picture. War books so often leave them out.
— Colonel T. E. Lawrence

The true leader never assumes anything, if he can possibly avoid it. Most of all, he never indulges in conventional wisdom—assuming that something is true just because everyone else assumes it.

Conventional wisdom is no wisdom at all. Conventional wisdom is taking somebody else's word for the way things are. And relying on somebody else's version of reality is about as smart as letting somebody else pack your parachute.

It's the *followers* in this world who rely on assumptions. Not the leaders.

In boot camp, they ought to break down the word "assume" into a marching cadence: "A-S-S-U-M-E! Assume makes an *ASS* out of *U* and *ME!*"

There are innumerable problems with making assumptions. One is that when people assume things, they generally think that everyone else—including their own team, as well as the enemy—is making the same assumption. However, people *rarely* agree on what the "facts" of any given situation are. We all like to think that we see things accurately and objectively, but that in *itself* is a faulty assumption.

Think I'm wrong? Think you have a good fix on the world as it is? Okay, then try a little experiment. Do you *assume* that you know what a penny looks like? Are you a reliable eyewitness on even that one simple thing? Then tell me the eight things that are pictured or written on every penny. Can you even name *four* or *five* of them? Probably not. The average person is only able to name three.

(Just so you won't have to dig one out of your pocket, here they are: Lincoln's face, the Lincoln Memorial, "One Cent," "In God We Trust," the date, "E Pluribus Unum," "United States of America," and "Liberty.")

An unreliable memory isn't the only thing that makes people see things differently. Perception is the easiest thing in the *world* to manipulate. I'll give you an example. A large group of people were shown a film of two cars colliding. Then they were broken into two groups. One group was asked, "How fast were the cars going when they crashed?" The other was asked, "How fast were the cars going when they made contact?" The group that heard the word "crash" assumed, on average, that the cars were going 40 mph. The ones that heard "contact" assumed 30 mph. Both groups thought they were making objective, rational assumptions, based only upon what they'd seen. But both were actually being manipulated by subliminal prejudice.

I've seen sailors on loading docks handle full gasoline drums with total care and attention, and then handle empty, vapor-filled gas drums with reckless abandon— even though they'd been *told* that empty drums were *more dangerous* than full drums. Why'd they act so stupidly? Because they just couldn't help but *assume* that the empty drums were actually safer. They couldn't get past their preconceived ideas. Maybe that's why they were lumpers on the dock, instead of officers.

Another problem with making assumptions is that assumptions rarely allow for the arrival of Mr. Murphy and *his* sick little bag of tricks. But be advised, the slimy bastard is out there, and he's just *waiting* for you and all your clever assumptions. You know that favorite phrase of big government and big business: "cost overruns"? When do you ever hear about cost "underruns"? Never. Because the people who make all the assumptions— even the "objective" bean counters who do the budget projections—have been lulled into complacency by our overinstitutionalized society. Mr. Murphy? Never heard of him.

What lulls these people into forgetting about Murphy? Simple. It's not their money. They don't care.

But even if you run a small business—and it *is* your money, and you *do* care—you're *still* likely to make half-assed assumptions, based on rosy projections. How come? Because you just don't have the heart to coldly face facts. If you told yourself the truth—that everything that *can* go wrong *will* go wrong—you'd probably never have the guts to try *anything*.

You probably regard optimism as a healthy trait. Maybe it is in your *personal* life—but in business, it's dangerous as hell. In business, optimism is a good trait for salesmen, because they can infect their buyers with it and make sales. But to a manager, it's a vice—just another unfounded assumption. Managers can't be optimists; they have to be *realists*. If managers make optimistic assumptions, they'll soon be up to their eyeballs in shit.

Let me tell you what happened to one manager. He made too many unfounded assumptions, drove a large business into bankruptcy, and put a bunch of families out into the cold. Then he died and promptly went to hell, for committing the sin of assumption. His first day in hell, the Devil greets him and says, "You've got a choice of three different places where you can spend eternity." Satan opens door number one: big room full of people getting kicked in the ass, one boot after another. Manager says, "What *else* have you got?" Satan opens door number two: big room of people getting slapped in the face—*smack*,

smack, smack! Nobody looks too happy. Manager says, "Maybe. But let's see room three." The Devil opens the door. It's a room full of people standing knee-deep in shit, holding cups and saucers and drinking coffee, while a gargoyle with a whip watches over them. The manager makes one last assumption—because this guy *never learns*. He assumes that he can tolerate the third room; the shit smells awful, but he *likes coffee*. So he tells the Devil, "I'll take room three." Door slams behind him. Deadbolts click shut. He's locked in for eternity. "Okay!" screams the gargoyle. "Coffee break's over! Back on your heads!"

The manager should have *asked more questions.* He shouldn't have assumed that the way things are *now* is the way they're *always* going to be.

Paul McCarthy, the brilliant and diligent editor of the Rogue Warrior autobiography and novels that I write with John Weisman, is a *master* of never assuming. He never assumes that a fact is true until he checks it. And he never assumes that the reader will understand something, just because he does. Therefore, Paul insists upon absolute clarity from John and me. There are a thousand ambitious editors in New York, but only a few at Paul's level—in part, because he has the discipline to *never assume.*

If you want to win your battles, let your *competition* make assumptions—and then find out what they are. If you know your enemy's assumptions, you have captured the element of surprise. And if you hold the element of surprise, you can determine the rules of engagement. You can control *where* you engage the enemy, *when* you engage them, and *how extensive* the battle will be.

To the extent that you *must* make assumptions, you should devise alternative plans to put in action if your assumptions prove to be false. You should always have a fallback position, a Plan B. If you're a true leader, even your backup systems will have backup systems.

Then, when your assumptions fall flat, you won't fall flat with them.

Stay flexible, and you'll win.

Be rigid, accept conventional wisdom, make assumptions—and you'll lose. I guarantee it.

The Rogue Warrior Mentality: Lessons from War

In the Vietnam War, the Pentagon's so-called best and brightest tried to "format" the war from three thousand miles away. After all, *they* had the fancy computers. Defense Secretary Robert McNamara thought he could churn out a military victory by using the same assembly-line methods he'd used at the Ford Motor Company. Stupid assumption. Cars and killing are two different businesses.

According to the assumptions of the armchair generals, those of us in the field would obediently follow their strict, rigid operational guidelines. Again, stupid assumption. When you're actually *out* there, getting your ass shot off, you sometimes take it upon yourself to vary the guidelines.

At least, I always did. Others didn't—and not all of them came home.

One guideline said that when we went out in riverboats

to curtail VC ambushes on the waterways, we were supposed to engage with the enemy until we had subdued him and then terminate the patrol—head home. On the face of it, that's a reasonable strategy; you do your job, call it quits, go to beer call, regroup, and live to fight another day.

Problem was, after we had followed this guideline for a few months, Victor Charles got the picture. He knew our patterns.

Knowing our assumptions and anticipating our rigid pattern, Charlie would see our PBR boat churning up the Bassac River, and he'd send out a decoy—some poor, luckless bastard who'd engage us in a little skirmish and who'd then either die, escape, or get captured. Then we'd chug home—as per format—assuming that we'd met the enemy and defeated him. Then the VC would get down to their real work. They'd move their troops and supplies across the river, unmolested.

Well, the day came when I could no longer abide by this idiocy. I did, after all, have a brain of my own, and I refused to assume that these weak-ass little attacks on us were bona fide.

One day, after that kind of decoy attack, I turned around and headed home.

Charlie assumed we were on our way back to base camp. As usual. So he started moving his supplies across the river.

When, much to his surprise, back roared Mr. Dick and his Merry Men. With Patches Watson at the throttle, we bore down on them, our dual 110-horsepower Mercury outboards churning at full blast and our starboard M60 machine guns blazing. Victor Chuck was caught with his pajamas down. Now *he* was the victim of assumptions. Charlie dropped his supplies in the water and ran like hell.

Around us, the water started to erupt in geysers, as bullets rained in. Suddenly, the SEAL next to me yelled and started to spout blood. I hurled him to the deck and yelled "Reverse!" We peeled out.

The firing drifted into the distance as we streaked home. I examined the man that was down. Superficial wound. Bloody but inconsequential.

We slowed our retreat as I bandaged him. Then I ordered us around again. In my gut, I knew Charlie was assuming the battle was over.

I was right. As we screamed down on them again, they looked up in utter shock: the element of surprise— I love it!

We did even more damage, then we got the hell out of there before Mr. Murphy could arrive.

On the way back, I steeled myself for the ass-chewing I knew I'd get. Successful or not, I'd violated the guidelines, and in that war, at that time, that was a no-no.

I knew that when the operations boss heard about our hijinks, he was going to wet his little pants. That much, I *did* assume.

And my assumption was quite correct. The boss had a fit. He couldn't see that we'd been *smart* to circumvent Charlie's assumptions.

After that, he was still the boss. But, in our eyes, he sure as hell wasn't the leader.

The Rogue Warrior Mentality: Lessons from Business

If any one man changed the face of America's entertainment industry—which is one of the few U.S. industries that still totally dominates all of its foreign rivals—that man is Lew Wasserman. Wasserman, the longtime head of the entertainment conglomerate MCA, is someone who never operated on assumptions if he could possibly help it. He hates them as much as I do.

Wasserman, who only recently phased out of MCA after about fifty years at the helm, was always the ultimate realist. He invariably looked beneath the obvious, and never accepted conventional wisdom.

MCA started out as just a talent agency—getting ten percent of the income of its movie star clients. Wasserman changed all that.

Until 1950 it had been assumed that in the movie business, the studio owners *owned* the movies and the stars *worked* in them. Wasserman questioned the validity of that assumption. As the talent agent for actor James Stewart, Wasserman demanded that Stewart have partial ownership of Stewart's [1953 movie, *Winchester 73*]. The film's studio—Universal—refused. They tried to bulldoze Stewart into taking the standard deal. But it hadn't been that long since Stewart had been in the war, risking his ass in real life and real-time, and he just didn't *bulldoze* very easily. Wasserman and Stewart were adamant. They raised holy hell. Universal caved. Stewart ended up making six hundred thousand dollars from that movie, about

115

twice as much as salaried superstars like Clark Gable got for a movie.

Another assumption Wasserman wouldn't accept was that talent agencies, like MCA, couldn't also produce movies themselves. Conventional wisdom held that this just wouldn't work—too many conflicting interests. But Wasserman started doing it, and MCA became tremendously powerful and successful working "both sides of the fence," as seller *and* buyer. Soon, MCA no longer had to negotiate with Universal, because Wasserman *bought* Universal.

Then Wasserman violated another "inviolable" assumption and increased his power and wealth geometrically. He stopped assuming that TV networks and production companies had the right of full ownership of their programs. Wasserman said that if the MCA talent agency supplied the major elements of a TV show—such as its star and its director—MCA should receive a full ten percent of that show's entire budget. In effect, he was demanding ten percent ownership of *dozens* of lucrative TV shows. When this "package fee" system was finally accepted—over the "dead bodies" of a few network execs—it enriched Wasserman and MCA beyond all imagining.

Wasserman, furthermore, was obsessed with protecting his own operating plans. He was determined to stay one step ahead of both the studios and the other talent agencies, by knowing their assumptions without letting them know his. He ordered his people to *never* put anything on paper unless they absolutely had to. At MCA, memos were rare, and it was against the rules to leave messages on a desk overnight (even when the only people around to see them were other MCA agents). Wasserman wouldn't even allow MCA agents to discuss business in public places, like restaurants. Wasserman also had intelligence-gathering operatives at each of the studios and networks. Often, Wasserman knew about a studio's projects even before the studio's own vice president knew about them.

One legendary story about Wasserman reveals his contempt for people who make assumptions.

Once, Wasserman had hired a new office assistant— someone to handle his errands, help answer his phone, and track his paperwork. This was a coveted position, because Wasserman's assistants often graduated to become full-fledged agents, who made hundreds of thousands of dollars a year. Wasserman's assistants were typically high-pedigree young men on the rise.

Wasserman's newest assistant was every bit as ambitious as his predecessors had been. He started early, finished late, and left no detail untended.

Quickly, the new assistant learned the patterns of the job. One of them was that every afternoon, Wasserman's secretary would tell him that Wasserman wanted him to drive to Wasserman's house to pick up a clean shirt, for use that evening. Wasserman wore the same "uniform" every day of his career: dark gray suit, white Sulka shirt, and thin black tie.

One afternoon the young assistant, while picking up the shirt, took an extra one, folded it carefully, covered it, and placed it in the trunk of his car. That way, when Wasserman requested the shirt the following day, the young man could run down to his car, grab it, and be back almost immediately. This efficiency, he assumed, would win the approval of Wasserman. It was a logical assumption.

The next day arrived, the request for the shirt came, and the assistant sprinted down to his car and returned momentarily. He handed the shirt to Wasserman's secretary.

Five minutes later, the secretary came to him and asked how he'd gotten the shirt so quickly. He told her, and she went off to report his answer to Wasserman.

The assistant was beaming. He was certain he'd made an impression. He allowed himself the luxury of stopping to drink a cup of coffee.

Minutes later, the secretary came out and told him that he was fired.

He couldn't believe it. "Why?"

"Because Mr. Wasserman wants you to do what he *wants*—not what you *think* he wants."

Coffee break was over.

Thus endeth the lesson: *Never assume.*

Chapter Nine

THE NINTH COMMANDMENT

"Verily, thou art not paid for thy methods, but for thy results, by which meaneth thou shalt kill thine enemy by any means available before he killeth you."

He who fails has no friends.

—Turkish proverb

Whoever wills the end, wills also the means.

—Immanuel Kant

Whenever I ask someone to do something important for me, and they fail, I don't want to *hear* about how they did their "best." Fuck their best. I want *results*.

If their best isn't good enough, it's up to them to *make it better*.

These days, a lot of people seem to think that it's not

121

whether you win or lose; it's how you play the game. Oh, yeah? Then why keep score?

Corporate managers today often believe all they have to do is just "give it the good old college try." They *don't* focus on results, and they *won't* take personal responsibility for their company's *overall success or failure.*

Part of the reason we see this lack of personal responsibility is that we've let our companies get too bureaucratized and compartmentalized. Everybody feels cut off from the "big picture."

Another reason this attitude is so common is simply that most people today shun responsibility. They *refuse* to take the blame when things go wrong, even if that means they won't get to take the credit when things go right. They'd rather just be *safe* and *snug*, and tiptoe their way through life.

A leader, though, should make everyone feel responsible for the success or failure of the entire team. If the team succeeds, *everybody* on it should feel like a hero; if it fails, everybody should feel like a goat.

If your team does fail, because of their own shortcomings, you shouldn't be afraid to punish them. Usually the best punishment is a quick and simple ass-chewing. Tell them exactly what they did wrong, and that you hold them personally responsible for their failure. After they get the point, *drop* it, completely and forever. The idea is to inspire a sense of individual responsibility in your people—*not* to make them feel like whipped dogs.

If you do inspire a sense of personal responsibility in your team, your people won't even *bother* to come to you with a bunch of excuses for failure. They'll just keep plugging away until they turn failure into success. They'll do *whatever it takes* to win.

I'm not saying you should make your people feel that the ends always justify the means. They don't. Your people must have a strong sense of right and wrong. If they don't, the environment inside your company will soon become cutthroat and chaotic.

But people *can* play by the rules and still *win.*

You have to make sure, though, that the rules you set are fair, sensible, and realistic. If your rules favor one type of employee over another, or if they don't conform to common sense, or if they're impossible to follow, no one will pay attention to them. You'll lose control. Your battle will turn into a disorganized free-for-all.

While you're being reasonable about rules, you also have to be reasonable about rewards. If your people get results, *reward* them. You have to use the "stick" *and* the "carrot."

If you make rewards big enough, people will do *anything* to get the results you want.

Reward success. Punish failure. Enforce responsibility. Insist on results. Do all this, and you'll turn your "group" into a *team.*

The Rogue Warrior Mentality: Lessons from War

The first thing I did when I arrived in the hellhole of Beirut, Lebanon, was to put my driver on commission. I paid him a fifty-dollar bonus each time we crossed through the battle zone without getting hit. I wanted him to have *every incentive* to survive.

Because I was in Beirut as an antiterrorist specialist, I knew the city was being terrorized by car bombs. By the time I'd been there for a couple of weeks, I'd heard ten car bombs go off. Hell of a noise. Load a big family sedan with 250 pounds of explosives and 250 pounds of scrap metal, and you've got yourself one big cherry bomb.

Car bombs scared the shit out of the populace because a car bomb could turn up *anywhere*.

It didn't take me long to figure out that car bombs were the biggest threat to the American Embassy in Beirut. If a terrorist could just get his car close to the embassy, *BAMM!*—blood in the hallways.

Protecting the embassy wasn't my responsibility—but fuck that. I didn't need an *invitation* to help.

So I figured out a way to protect the embassy. I got in touch with some military munitions design engineers and asked them to make me a device that would detonate a car bomb by remote control. Most of the bombs were activated by an electronic signal; when the terrorists transmitted a pulse on a certain frequency, it set off their bomb.

My engineering contacts sent me a device that would transmit on a broad band of frequencies. It would detonate any bomb within a thousand yards. With this device, a guard could just sit on the roof of the embassy and blow a terrorist to hell before he even got close.

Me being me, I had to try it out. I decided to go cruising with a couple of buddies. We hopped in a car with the device and with a specially designed "briefcase" that was actually a Heckler & Koch submachine gun.

We drove into an area of West Beirut that was controlled by the Palestine Liberation Organization. We parked in front of a burned-out building that had recently been Yasir Arafat's office. We activated the device.

Suddenly, about a block away, a building rocked with noise and flame. Its roof shot straight up and its walls spewed into the street. It was obviously a bomb factory.

Instantly, the entire area was filled with Lebanese punks carrying guns. We got the hell out of there before anyone could shoot us.

I reported immediately to one of the military commanders of the embassy and told him about my device.

He looked at me as if I was crazy.

First, he informed me, the security of the embassy was not my problem. And none of my business.

Second, he was concerned that if a car bomb was detonated unexpectedly, it might violate State Department rules by killing innocent civilians.

"But what about innocent *Americans?*" I said.

He cut me off. Wouldn't listen. According to *his* rules, my device was "unfair."

I suggested that American lives were more important than "his" rules. I suggested that he refocus on *results* and not *rules.* That just pissed him off.

He tossed my ass out of his office.

Soon after, I left town. I took my radio device with me.

About three months after I left, a truck filled with explosives drove up in front of the American Embassy and blew it to pieces. Sixty-three Americans died. Many more were maimed.

The commander was not injured.

He lived to "lead" again.

Hopefully, after that, he felt a greater sense of personal responsibility for his people, and worried more about *results* than about *rules.*

But I doubt it.

The Rogue Warrior Mentality: Lessons from Business

When Michael Eisner took over the ailing Disney entertainment company in the mid-1980s, he refused to follow the "rules" that governed Hollywood.

He refused to pay movie stars the huge fees that they demanded. Eisner's second-in-command, Jeff Katzenberg, vowed, "We have the money, but we won't pay retail."

Stars, of course, reacted venomously. They predicted that Eisner would die a quick and painful corporate death.

Eisner broke another long-standing Hollywood rule when he decreed that Disney film executives should start coming up with their *own* movie ideas, instead of following the traditional route of waiting for directors, writers, and producers to come up with concepts. This, too, angered the creative community. But it promised to save a great deal of money.

Most unorthodox of all, Eisner rejected the standard hefty salary that other studio heads were getting. Instead, he bargained for a big back-end payoff—*if* Disney succeeded. He took an option to purchase 510,000 shares of company stock. Eisner wanted to gamble on *results*—and not just the results of *his* performance, but of his *company's*.

Disney began originating their own film ideas, and casting them with talented actors who were in career slumps. For example, they put Richard Dreyfuss, Nick Nolte, and Bette Midler—all of whom were then perceived as "washed up"—in *Down and Out in Beverly Hills*. Disney then got two TV actors, Tom Selleck and Ted Danson, to appear in *Three Men and a Baby*. The company also began making new animated features, like *Who Framed Roger Rabbit*; these movies had very low "talent" costs.

Disney's movie expenditures averaged $12 million—compared to the industry average of $16.5 million.

Disney's movies were hits. *Big hits*. Hollywood's "old rules" apparently didn't make much sense.

Within a few years, Disney was by far the most successful entertainment company in the world. It still is.

By betting on the overall success of his own company, Michael Eisner became quite wealthy. His stock options and bonuses ended up being worth well over $100 million.

Eisner had been unorthodox. He had rejected the existing rules and had created newer, smarter rules.

He had focused on *results*.

He had taken full personal responsibility. And he had reaped a full financial reward.

Michael Eisner had proved that, even in Hollywood, it's possible to have a Rogue Warrior mentality.

* * *

IBM was one of the first major companies to begin paying a wage that was based entirely on productivity.

In 1958 IBM abolished the standardized hourly-wage system for all its employees, including production workers. Everyone was put on a salary. The salary was based strictly on productivity. Not seniority. Not effort. Not title. Just *results*.

Shortly after that, IBM gave *every one* of its employees a stock purchase plan. Anyone who worked for IBM could use up to ten percent of his or her salary to buy IBM stock at fifteen percent below market value. Virtually all of the employees who took full advantage of the program retired as millionaires. They bet on the results of their own company—and they won.

In 1992 Dana Mead, a former West Point professor, took over the troubled Tenneco natural gas company. The company was plagued by corporate infighting and by lack of acceptance of managerial responsibility. Mead wanted to institute changes that would be, in his words, "quick and violent." He adopted a "no excuses" policy. His "mantra," as he put it, was "*Results*, not best efforts." He inaugurated a new bonus plan in which all top-level bonuses were based fifty percent on the ability to lead change. He also started a brutally honest peer-review program.

After these changes, Tenneco emerged with lower overhead costs, higher profits, and a reinvigorated workforce. These few, simple adjustments gave the corporation a whole new success-oriented mind-set.

Chapter Ten

THE TENTH COMMANDMENT

"Thou shalt, in thy Warrior's Mind and Soul, always remember My ultimate and final Commandment: There Are No Rules—Thou Shalt Win at All Cost."

When you have them by the balls, their hearts and minds will follow.

—Vietnam veterans' proverb

He who overcomes an enemy by fraud is as much to be praised as he who does so by force.

—Niccolò Machiavelli

Conventionality is not morality.

—Charlotte Brontë

Following conventional wisdom is *not wise.* It's just following the rules that *other people* have made. To be a leader, you've got to make your *own* rules.

To win a battle, you should dictate the "rules of engagement." If you let your enemy decide the rules that will govern the battle, he will devise rules that will favor him. If you dictate the rules of engagement, you'll take control.

When somebody tells me that they "love a fair fight," I know they're a loser. The last thing I want is for my fights to be fair. I want them to be as lopsided and unequal as possible—in my favor, of course. If I can't stack the deck, I'll wait until I do have an advantage: then I'll attack.

I'm not saying that a leader should be unprincipled and break the rules of common decency. As you know, I believe a leader should adhere to a high moral code. You need to follow principles to keep your team cohesive, and to keep your people as loyal to your cause as they are to you.

However, you can be true to your principles and still make your own rules. You can't get stuck in the rut of doing what everyone else is doing, just because that's the path of least resistance. You've got to blaze your own trails. Innovate. Create. Improvise. Your goal is to always win. And that may mean doing whatever it takes to win.

You have to do whatever you can to avoid stale patterns of action. When you follow predictable patterns, your people will stop thinking and go on automatic pilot. And your enemy will know exactly what to expect from you.

One way to break yourself of the habit of following everybody else's rules is to create situations where you and your people have to be creative to win. For example, imagine that you and your team have set a goal of climbing to the top of a mountain. But by the time you're halfway up the mountain, you realize you can't safely climb down. There is now only one way to go: up. You have just created what I call the no-option option. Your only option is success. To achieve it, you'll *have* to improvise; you'll simply have no other option.

The Irish have a proverb that goes, When two young men reach a wall they can't climb over, they should throw their caps over the wall—because then, to keep from losing their caps, they've *got* to climb the wall.

When Jack Kennedy—who ordered the creation of the SEALs—was gearing up to send a man to the moon, he quoted that proverb, saying that America had to "throw its cap over the wall of space." It was his last challenge to America. The day after he said it, he was assassinated. But America committed itself to that project, difficult as it seemed at the time, and took the creative steps necessary to carry out the mission.

As a leader, you've got to go where no man has gone before. Take the point. Screw the "rules." Just win.

The Rogue Warrior Mentality: Lessons from War

In the Delta area of Vietnam, our River Patrol Division commanding officer got in the habit of sending out search-and-destroy patrols into the bush every day just after daybreak. He would usually send them up the primary existing trail or canal.

Almost every day, the patrol would then meet with the enemy, get shot to shit, and drag ass back home.

The reason they got massacred was that they were invariably *ambushed*. After all, it was Charlie's bush, so he had the advantage of setting the rules of engagement.

Almost always, we killed more of Victor Charles than

he did of us, because we had superior firepower and communications. Therefore, the CO thought he was a very astute military tactician. He did, indeed, boast a very high body count—and that's how success was measured in that war. The conventional wisdom at the Pentagon was that if we got way ahead of Charlie on "points," Chuck would just give up. I know that's not very smart, but conventional wisdom rarely is.

I sat down with the CO and, in my usual diplomatic way, broached the subject of his absolute *idiocy*. After all, I reasoned, why *shouldn't* Charlie bushwhack us every day, since we were almost always in the same place at the same time? Wouldn't it be better *etiquette*, I asked, for us to just send Charlie an *invitation*, so he'd know exactly where and when to come kick our ass? That way, he could spend more quality time with Mrs. Charlie and the kids.

From that cordial chat, I did obtain permission to run a patrol of my own. The idea was to go ambush Charlie before he could ambush us.

On the day of the mission, we went out in camouflage at 0200, long before light, and cut straight through the bush, avoiding all trails. It was slow and painful, but at least we didn't run into any "surprise parties."

By 0545, as first light was turning the sky opaque, we were hunkered on a hilltop that looked out over the main trail. In fifteen minutes, our Provisional Reconnaissance Unit patrol, or PRU, would be moving up that trail. The idea of the game was to spot Charlie before he could move against our patrol, and throw down on him with serious ordnance. We were going to ambush the ambush.

Our fallback position—if we couldn't spot Charlie *before* the ambush—was to move in behind him after the firefight started and catch him in a "pincer movement."

My radioman, who was in touch with the PRU patrol, signaled me that they were approaching. I signaled my men to stand ready.

Then, suddenly, *whap! whap! whap!* The ground around us exploded in puffs of dust. Shit! We were being ambushed! Somehow, Charlie had gotten wind of us, and now he had us outflanked.

If I didn't do something immediately, about half my men were soon going to be nothing more than bundles in body bags.

I wanted to do the most unpredictable thing imaginable. If we followed standard operating procedure and dug in, we were going to get butchered.

"Attack!" I screamed. I hurtled toward the sound of the gunfire. "Attack! *Attack! ATTACK!*"

With me leading from the front, my men—my warriors—fell in behind, shrieking like banshees and laying down automatic-weapon fire that was as thick as a wave of flame.

We ambushed the ambush. I hadn't learned this tactic from any military textbook. But I knew it was time to throw out the rules, opt for the no-option option, and just *win*.

Our "crazy" attack shocked the shit out of Charlie.

The VC scattered.

Most of them disappeared into the bush, but we herded a few of them into our advancing PRU patrol down below.

None of my men were killed. None were wounded.

We'd broken the usual patterns and rejected the old rules. We'd exercised the no-option option. When we'd attacked the ambush, our only choice had been: succeed or die.

We had succeeded. They had died.

And that's how all good war stories end.

The Rogue Warrior Mentality: Lessons from Business

In World War II, the bloody battle of Okinawa was won with the help of two kids from Pennsylvania, Jack McCloskey and his buddy Stan Novak. Both were big-shot college athletes who had willingly left the glamour of Ivy League sports to enlist in the Navy. McCloskey, in fact, was the youngest skipper in the armed services, commanding a landing craft at age nineteen.

Forty-five years later, they were still "fighting" together, battling for a world championship in the National Basketball Association. McCloskey was the general manager of the Detroit Pistons, and Novak was his chief scout and top adviser.

McCloskey had been an NBA coach or general manager for decades, but a championship had always eluded him, as it does most GMs. It was the law of averages: twenty-seven teams, but only one winner. He'd gotten close before—but to McCloskey, close didn't count.

Midway through the 1989 season, though, McCloskey

and Novak were tantalizingly close. The Pistons had an excellent team, mostly because McCloskey had ignored conventional wisdom about what it took to win in the NBA. He had created his own rules of success.

For many years, it had been considered imperative to build your team around the center position. All the champions of the 1970s and 1980s had had talented, inspiring centers, like Kareem Abdul-Jabbar, Moses Malone, Robert Parish, and Bill Walton. But McCloskey's center was Bill Laimbeer, a slow, sunken-chested misanthrope.

McCloskey, instead, had put his offensive firepower in his guards—the little guys.

The little guys, however, didn't score exceptionally well, so McCloskey got creative again and decreed that his team would win *without* a powerful offense. They'd stress *defense*. That was heresy, but it worked. The team's attacking, swarming defense was spectacular and earned the team the nickname "The Bad Boys." But that "negative" nickname didn't bother McCloskey at all. He *liked* having the other teams thinking that when they played the Pistons, they were going to get their asses kicked around. It distracted them and usually made them play macho, Piston-style ball. Thus, the Pistons dictated the rules of engagement.

Furthermore, McCloskey built a team that had only two star players, Isiah Thomas and Adrian Dantley. Conventional wisdom dictated that he needed more. But that's not how McCloskey saw it. He thought the *opposite*.

Three months before the playoffs, McCloskey invoked a

strategy that he called "addition by subtraction." He wanted to add to his team by subtracting its leading scorer, Adrian Dantley.

McCloskey believed there were just two elements that made teams great. The first was "mix"—having players with *complementary* skills. The second was "chemistry"—having players who respected and trusted each other. McCloskey thought Dantley wasn't good for his team's mix and chemistry.

When word got around the league that McCloskey was looking to trade Dantley, a number of "experts" thought he was crazy. The Pistons were only a few games out of first place, and if the trade didn't propel the team to a championship, McCloskey would be branded as "the man who traded away the title." He'd probably lose his job.

But McCloskey had no particular fear of risk. Whenever he began to feel nervous, he'd think back to the days when he'd ridden out typhoons in the South Pacific. When he did that, life in the NBA didn't feel quite so perilous.

McCloskey lined up a trade. He wanted to pick up small-forward Mark Aguirre. Again, the reigning "wisdom" around the league held that trading for Aguirre would be nuts. Aguirre was a lifetime misfit, a talented player who had never been able to get along with his teammates.

But McCloskey felt he could handle Aguirre. If Aguirre acted up, McCloskey was quite prepared to *personally kick Aguirre's ass*, if that's what it took.

Because Dantley was a local favorite, public opinion was strongly opposed to McCloskey "pulling the trigger" on the Dantley-Aguirre trade.

But McCloskey made the deal. Shortly afterward he noted, "It was a calculated risk. I knew that from the beginning. But you look at it this way and that, and analyze it from every angle. You do your homework, and you don't let public opinion enter into it. You just agonize over it.

"Then, after all that, you just pick up the gun. You pick up the gun and pull the damn trigger."

The first day Aguirre practiced with the team, its strongest player smashed into Aguirre with brutal intensity. It was, in fact, the intensity McCloskey had cultivated in the team—the intensity he insisted on. Aguirre crumpled to the floor. For a second, he was just a big pile of meat. Then he stirred and began to take a more human shape. Isiah Thomas strolled over. "Welcome to the Pistons," he said.

From the day of Aguirre's first game, the trade paid off. Aguirre quickly became the team's leading scorer. And on McCloskey's team, he behaved himself.

The Pistons won the championship that year. And the next year, too.

McCloskey had achieved his ultimate goal because he had been brave enough to make a change. He'd "broken the rules" of conventional wisdom and had blazed his own trail.

Jack McCloskey, the Rogue Warrior of the NBA, had shown that if you ignore conventional wisdom and make your own rules, you can win. Twice.

Maintaining the leadership edge: six questions to ask yourself daily

Now that you've read the book, I want you to ask yourself, What did I *learn* from this?

If your honest answer is: Nothing!—then take the book back to the bookstore. Give it to the clerk—and have him smack the shit out of you with it. Maybe that will knock some sense into you.

There's no excuse for not learning valuable lessons from this book, because the principles in it came from real-time *war*, not from some think tank—and if the principles did *not* work, I would not be *alive*. It's as simple as that.

As you may remember, in the beginning of the book I told you that there are six questions that I ask myself virtually every morning. These are the questions that I use to focus my purpose and to understand *myself* and my *mission*.

If I find that I'm *unable* to adequately answer these questions—within the context of that day's mission—then I know that either I'm *on the wrong mission* or there's *something wrong with me*.

These six questions are: **What drives me? Was I always this way? What will satisfy me? Do I ever recognize defeat? How can I turn today's negatives into positives? What is my ultimate goal?**

When you first saw these questions in the Introduction, you may have had your own answers for them. *Now*, though, if you've learned anything from my Ten Commandments of leadership success, you should have somewhat *different* answers to these questions.

For your first "training mission" as a warrior, let's go over these questions one at a time. I'll tell you my answers to them, all of which stem from elements of my Ten Commandments. If you didn't sleepwalk through this book, my Ten Commandments will now help you formulate some of your answers, too.

What drives me? In every mission I'm on, the thing that drives me most is the desire to *find my limits*—and *extend* them.

144

I don't embark on a mission in hopes of discovering how *little* I can do and still "get by." Instead, I lead from the front and explore new areas of myself, my values, my beliefs, and my environment—in every mission I accept. By doing this, I constantly learn where my current limits are and how I can surpass them.

The only way to truly "take the point" on a mission—and discover new aspects of yourself—is to leave fear and doubt behind. Doing *that* is simply a matter of will. It may not be something you will *like* doing. It's something you just *do*.

In exploring new territories of myself, I have discovered that virtually every internal limitation I have—such as a temporary inability to learn a new skill—has been created by *my own mind*. I have spent many solitary hours—in the jungles of Southeast Asia and the deserts of the Middle East—pondering my own subjective limitations. And I have found that practically *no* realistic goal is impossible for me to achieve unless I have *convinced* myself it's impossible.

If I ignore pain, punish myself in training, and keep my tactics simple, I find that, often as not, I am able to "do the impossible."

My ability to "do the impossible" is magnified tremendously when I define "me" as *my team and I*. When you merge with a team of warriors, your fear fades, and your capabilities increase geometrically. When you learn to expand yourself by "becoming one" with a team, you personally incorporate all of the strengths of all of your team members. When you add this collective strength to your own, you become virtually "superhuman."

145

Now, ask yourself, "What drives me?"

Was I always this way? No. Every new day changes me. Every mission changes me. And every new team changes me.

If you're not actively involved in constantly re-creating yourself, then you're actively involved in *stagnating*. The minute you're born, you begin to die. But if you give in to the process of constant stagnation, you die "a thousand deaths."

My life in the SEALs, my command of SEAL Team Six, and my leadership of Red Cell *made* me the man I am.

In order to change in a positive way, though, you've *first* got to know exactly who you are. The best way to learn exactly who you are, and what you're made of, is to accept responsibility for the lives of other men—and to place *your* life in *their* hands. When you do this, you *quickly* learn to define yourself—with *extreme* clarity. Then, once you fully understand the foundation of your own character, you are able to make changes constructively.

Of course, your identity shifts somewhat each time you accept a new mission and each time you work with a new team. And as your missions and teammates change, you discover the full spectrum of your personality and character. Sometimes you like what you discover, and sometimes you don't. When you don't like what you see in yourself, it hurts. But that hurt is *good*, because it lets you know you're being completely honest with yourself, and it tells you to *change something*. Remember, when you hurt, you're "doing it right."

You don't have to be in a war, though, to learn about

146

yourself. You just have to be a serious person with a serious mission. As a kid, I began to change just from simple childhood experiences. When I was five, and peddled papers with my uncles, I learned how to "sell myself" to other people. That changed me. When I stayed in the Catskill Mountains with my aunt and uncle during the summers of my grade-school years, I learned to love adventure—and that changed me *forever*. When I was twelve, and started working in a bowling alley, I learned to be independent. And when I was fourteen, and started working up to eighty hours a week in a luncheonette, I learned to endure tough work. All of these changes helped me to learn. The most *important* thing I learned was that the smarter I got, the dumber I realized I was.

If you don't change at least a little on every one of your missions, you're just going through the motions.

Ask yourself: How have *I* changed recently?

What will satisfy me? For me, total satisfaction will come only when I completely merge my full potential with my *actions*.

It isn't enough to just *know* your full potential; you have to get your ass out on the battlefield and *reach* your potential, with balls-to-the-wall action.

If you don't try to do this every day, you'll soon be just another windbag with warmed-over war stories.

Once in a while, I get tempted to sit back and gloat about my accomplishments over a couple of drinks of Bombay gin. Whenever that happens, I force myself to snap back to reality. Reality is, discipline is an *everyday process*, and I *still* have a lot left to accomplish. And, God willing, I always will. The challenge ahead is what keeps me alive.

I have no patience with self-satisfied people who no longer work to their maximum abilities.

Every morning when we wake up, we're all equal: we all face the exact same risk of stagnating, *unless* we challenge ourselves. We've all got to keep challenging ourselves, again and again, each new day.

Sound hard? It is. Sound impossible? It's *not*.

I am still growing in knowledge and in purpose. The world has opened many doors of opportunity for me. Each new opportunity gives me the chance to test myself and my beliefs, to discover truth, and to continue to prove myself.

I hope I *never* stop growing.

It's quite probable that I'll never completely merge my full potential with my actions. Therefore, I'll probably never be totally satisfied. But I don't despair at this. I *glory* in it.

I am the War Lord of combat, and my battle will never end.

When will *you* be satisfied?

Do I ever recognize defeat? Hell, no! At least, not in the way most people look at defeat.

When I define defeat, I break it down into its two root words: *de*, the Latin word that means "to go from," and *feat*, an English word meaning "accomplishment." Many times, of course, I've had "to go away from" what I hoped to "accomplish." But, to me, that meant I was *sidetracked*, not vanquished. I lived to fight another day.

Like Ernest Hemingway, I believe that "a man can be destroyed but not defeated."

One thing I hate particularly about the usual definition of defeat is that it implies that the defeated person has been overcome by an *outside force*—usually an enemy. But it's almost never your enemy who "defeats" you—it's *yourself.*

People just blithely assume that the main reason they don't achieve their goal is that someone *else* beat them to it. But remember, Thou shalt never assume. If you finish second, it's not *because* someone else finished first. That person's victory was just a "side effect" of your failure. If you lost, it was because you didn't sufficiently punish yourself in training, and didn't focus the full force of your being on victory. If you don't own up to that fact, then you won't be able to fully understand yourself—and you'll set yourself up for another failure. If you *do* own up to it, and learn from it, you'll be able to look your people in the eye, and lead them "from the front." Then you'll get your victory—the second time around.

All of your internal limitations—which are always what cause your failures—can be overcome. If you stay in the battle long enough, and refuse to give up, you'll soon be able to overcome your self-imposed limitations, and succeed. Your victory won't always put you in "first place," but if you push yourself to the ultimate, and overcome all of your internal limitations, you'll still be a winner. And if you're a winner, you probably *will* finish first—eventually.

To a warrior, defeat is a temporary condition. Set your course, and blow the obstacles out of the water!

Ask yourself, Do I ever recognize defeat?

149

* * *

How can I turn today's negatives into positives? I start by realizing that "negative" and "positive" are just labels—often used inaccurately.

When you decide what's negative and what's positive, you're probably being guided by the past. If something has been negative in the past, you assume that it's still negative. But that can be misleading. As missions change, so do negatives and positives. I *refuse* to be a slave to history. My history is just that, *history.* My focus is fixed on the future, and I don't *assume* that something will be negative now just because it has been in the past.

Everything changes. And if *you* don't change, you'll soon be just another old fart on the sidelines.

If I find that something truly *is* negative—that it has significantly hurt me or helped my enemy—I don't dwell on the damage. Instead, I ask myself: What can I *get* out of this?

Usually, even in a disaster, I can salvage something. If my jeep gets totaled, I'll pull out the engine, remove the radio, and grab anything else that still works.

Even if *everything* in a situation is destroyed, I'll still try to *learn* something from the experience. Often, the things I learn from a minor problem later prevent a major disaster.

Even when my enemy totally succeeds at achieving his goal, I don't accept it as a negative. I use *his* success for *my* education. I *copy* what he does. Then I do it *better.*

Another reason I try to avoid the traditional labels of positive and negative is that they tend to *complicate* things. If you strip away those labels, you simplify your approach

150

to your mission. If you're not worrying about positives and negatives, it's easier to focus just upon *what works* and what *doesn't work*. And when you do that, it vastly increases your chance of success.

If I'm faced with a worst-case scenario—a negative situation where nothing is salvageable and there's not even anything I can learn—I *still* use it to my advantage. How? I use it for *motivation*. I use it to spur myself and my men, by making it a challenge to our pride.

Ask yourself, Are *your* negatives *really* negative? If they are, what can you *salvage*? What can you *learn*? And how can you use it to *push* yourself?

Now let's consider the last, most fascinating question: **What is my ultimate goal?**

As a leader, it's absolutely imperative that you know exactly *what you want*—and how you plan to *get it*.

To me, understanding my ultimate goal is the key to understanding myself, because I can't define my goal unless I can first define exactly *who I am*.

In the military, I had the luxury of having an obvious goal. My ultimate goal was simple: *survival*. When people were doing their damnedest to kill me, I didn't have to *agonize* over the *complexities* of my goal in life.

However, even though my goal was not *complex*, that did not mean it was easily achieved. I came excruciatingly close to death many times.

However, by focusing *completely* on my ultimate goal of survival, I became acutely aware of how to fulfill that goal. I learned *how to be a survivor*.

I learned that the best way for me to attain my ultimate

goal of survival was by following my own Ten Commandments. These Ten Commandments, I found, were so sensible and so powerful that they applied to almost *anyone* who was trying to achieve his ultimate goal.

One of the first things I learned about survival is that it is not always your "enemies" who most jeopardize your life. Often, it is your "allies." Many times, I was put in harm's way by my own commanding officers, who sent me onto the field of battle hampered by illogical rules of engagement, outdated tactics, and unreliable equipment and weaponry.

Because of this, I soon realized that the best way for me to survive would be for me to fight my own battles in my own way. When I took over SEAL Team Six and Red Cell, that's exactly what I did.

Once I had my own units, I was freed from the rigid rules and policies that were designed to guide the "masses" of military men. I was also freed from having to work under incompetent commanding officers. I was able to fight like a *warrior*. I was able to take responsibility, show initiative, and do *whatever it took* to survive and succeed.

This *freedom to act* is what made SEAL Team Six and Red Cell so effective. It's what enabled us to survive and succeed.

When I commanded SEAL Six, we disregarded old ways of thinking. I led from the front, and I pushed my men severely in training. I remade them in my own "warrior image," and treated them all alike—just like shit—*until* they proved themselves.

The men in SEAL Six learned to push themselves past pain, and to focus only on results. They "played to win." And, ultimately, they became one of America's legendary combat forces.

The men in SEAL Six were the ultimate survivors. They never lost sight of their ultimate goal, and that's what made them winners.

The men in Red Cell were also masters of survival and masters of success.

In Red Cell, we didn't just sit around and *talk* about what a terrorist might do. We actually "became" terrorists, and learned to see the world as terrorists see it.

Military men who were not a part of Red Cell never really understood why we did the things we did. To them, our techniques always seemed "unfair" and "simplistic." In reality, our techniques were *unorthodox* and *uncomplicated*. That's why they succeeded. And that's why we survived.

After I left the Navy, I found that there are millions of people in America today who are struggling to survive and succeed, in their careers and in their personal lives.

And in many ways, the world they live in—the job world and modern society—is just as unforgiving, ruthless, and venal as the world of combat.

Therefore, I found that many of the same rules I learned in war also helped people in normal daily life to survive and succeed—and to achieve their ultimate goal, no matter what it was.

For example, I discovered that often it is not your business competitors who are your biggest threat—it is your associate in the office next door. Maybe he wants your job, or maybe he's just a dumb-ass manager who doesn't know how to give you the support you need to survive.

And it's also brutal *outside* your own company. When you leave your building and navigate the "jungles" of the business world, you quickly discover that there is only one governing principle—survival of the fittest. Today's global business competitors can be as hostile as enemy snipers, and as unpredictable as terrorists.

Their goal is to kill your company before it kills theirs. They are quite willing to destroy you by any means available. They are willing to push their subordinates unmercifully. They are willing to endure pain, to break rules, and to sacrifice bravely until they dominate you.

To survive, you must know how they think, what they value, what they expect—and what they know about *you.*

If your ultimate goal is to survive and succeed in your career and in your personal life, you've got to be tougher, more motivated, and more focused than *anybody* who might stand between you and your goal.

If you want to be a survivor and a winner, you must set your eyes on goals that are as lofty as the *heavens.* And you must sit your *ass* in the *gutter*—so that you can get down to the dirty work that victory *demands.*

You must attack your competitors in ways that will be so surprising that even *you* will be surprised.

You must attack your competitors even when they "ambush" you.

You must attack the laziness, weakness, and complacency of your subordinates—because that is the only way to build a team of warriors.

You must attack your self-imposed internal limitations—because that's the first step to being a leader.

You must learn to attack each new day with vigor, optimism, and a profound belief in a personal cause.

You must attack the jobs you *hate* with even more zest than the jobs you *love*.

You must learn to attack your training regimen with joy and devotion.

To survive and succeed, you must accept one plain and painful truth: Business can be *war*. *Life* can be war.

If you want to *win* that war:

Attack.

Attack!

ATTACK!